The Best of **WOODCARVING** ILLUSTRATED

POWER CARVING
MANUAL UPDATED & EXPANDED
Second Edition

The Best of **WOODCARVING** ILLUSTRATED

POWER CARVING
MANUAL UPDATED & EXPANDED Second Edition

Tools, Techniques &
22 All-Time
Favorite Projects

With contributions by Frank Russell,
Jack Kochan, Lori Corbett, Chuck Solomon,
and Dave Hamilton

**Reciprocating tools recreate
the look of a handcarved
project. See page 21.**

FOX CHAPEL
PUBLISHING

© 2018 by Fox Chapel Publishing Company, Inc., 903 Square Street, Mount Joy, PA 17552.

Power Carving Manual, Updated & Expanded Second Edition (2018) is a revised edition of *Power Carving Manual* (2009), published by Fox Chapel Publishing Company, Inc. Revisions include updated tool recommendations and pricing, and new projects. The patterns contained herein are copyrighted by the authors and Fox Chapel Publishing, Inc. Readers may make copies of these patterns for personal use. The patterns themselves, however, are not to be duplicated for resale or distribution under any circumstances. Any such copying is a violation of copyright law.

ISBN 978-1-56523-903-6

Library of Congress Cataloging-in-Publication Data

Title: Power carving manual.
Other titles: Woodcarving illustrated.
Description: Updated and expanded second edition. | Mount Joy [Pennsylvania]
 : Fox Chapel Publishing, [2018] | Includes index.
Identifiers: LCCN 2017044300 | ISBN 9781565239036 (pbk.)
Subjects: LCSH: Wood-carving. | Power tools.
Classification: LCC TT199.7 .P675 2018 | DDC 736/.4--dc23
LC record available at https://lccn.loc.gov/2017044300

To learn more about the other great books from Fox Chapel Publishing, or to find a retailer near you,
call toll-free 800-457-9112 or visit us at *www.FoxChapelPublishing.com*.

We are always looking for talented authors. To submit an idea, please send a brief inquiry to
acquisitions@foxchapelpublishing.com.

Printed in Singapore
Third printing

Welcome

Woodcarving Illustrated magazine presents this collection of power carving articles and resources. Whether you're just getting started in power carving or have been using power carving tools for years, the following pages offer resources and projects you'll want to turn to again and again.

This book is divided into three sections. The first section goes over the basics of safety, tools, accessories, and anything else you'll need to set up a work area and get started. If you're just beginning in power carving, you'll want to start with the first section. The second section is a set of articles focused on techniques, from basic cuts to texturing feathers. The last section offers projects to try out your newly learned techniques, hone your existing skills, or simply find inspiration for your next carving project.

Contents

103

85

157

114

95

102

Projects

120

91

Getting Started

Carving with power involves the use of motorized equipment that rotates a shaft with a cutting bur mounted on the end. Because the rotating bur grinds away wood in a very controlled manner, power carving allows you to create delicate designs and intricate details that would be extremely difficult to carve with traditional tools.

Contributors to this chapter include Dave Hamilton, Jack Kochan, Frank Russell, Roger Schroeder, and Chuck Solomon.

Carving a gunstock with an
air turbine tool, page 19.

The use of power tools became more common among carvers in the 1970s. About 90% of bird carvers use power for some or all of their carving. Carvers who specialize in mammals, fish, humans, and interpretative carvings also use power for carving.

In addition to affording you more control, power carving tools generally remove wood faster than traditional edge tools. They also let you create thin carvings and achieve highly detailed pieces. It is possible to accomplish similar effects using edge tools, but it is much more difficult. Power tools carve in areas, such as tight recesses, where it is nearly impossible to fit traditional tools. For example, it's much easier to create a delicate hummingbird bill without breaking it, when using power; however, one small slip with a knife or gouge and the bird's bill is destroyed. Power carving does not preclude the use of edge tools, but enhances your ability to achieve desired effects in your carving.

In addition to the effects possible with power carving tools, carving with power opens up a world of opportunities for carvers with arthritis

Power carvers can create thin delicate carvings. This hibiscus was carved by Wanda Marsh.

Power Carving Pros and Cons

Power carving offers several advantages over carving with hand tools, but there are drawbacks. It's important to weigh all of the factors involved and make an informed decision. When possible, experiment with the tools and techniques before investing in power carving equipment.

DRAWBACKS OF POWER CARVING

• Involves a higher initial investment

• Has specific safety concerns

• Creates noise

• Generates dust

BENEFITS OF POWER CARVING

• Removes wood quickly and with precision, especially when using hardwoods

• Minimizes splintering and fracturing of the wood

• Provides greater control than knives or gouges when carving fine detail

• Allows carving and grinding of metal and epoxies

• Provides quick and controlled sanding

• Eliminates the need for sharpening

• Provides an alternative for carvers who have difficulty with edge tools due to arthritis, etc.

or limited hand strength. You must be committed to taking the proper precautions when it comes to safety, but power carving offers rich rewards and can greatly enhance your enjoyment of carving wood.

Power carving can also be a boon to those who hate to sharpen. With power carving, you can easily carve the hardest woods without ever stopping to sharpen your tools.

If you've been thinking about using power tools for the first time or expanding your collection of power tools, this section can help you get started. Included here is what you'll need to know to set up a safe work environment, find the right tools, and select the right bits and accessories.

Safety

Safety is the first consideration of this book, and it should be for any shop or working area. All types of carving involve some risks. Being informed and taking the proper precautions will keep you safe and enhance your carving experience.

Most woodcarvers have at least a table saw or a radial arm saw to cut carving stock into manageable pieces, and a band saw for blanking out. Many also have a jointer and/or planer in addition to a drill press to smooth out and assist with different aspects of joinery. Every one of the machines mentioned has the capability of inflicting permanent and debilitating injuries, and care must be given to each machine in its turn with respect to safety through use, location, surrounding area, accessory use/storage, safety devices, electrical setup, blade guards/guides, and waste disposal.

It is not the scope of this book to consider safety aspects of large machinery, but I would feel remiss by not mentioning these areas of danger found in the shop or work area. Safety can never be overemphasized.

The primary safety considerations for power carving are the quiet but deadly ones: dust inhalation and fire hazard resulting from improper dust collection and disposal. We'll also discuss what safety items you should wear while carving.

Dust

The inhalation of dust is the biggest risk power carvers face. Cutting, grinding, and sanding all generate dust. The small particles of wood that remain in the air can cause respiratory problems when inhaled.

Asthma, allergic reactions, and long-term risks, such as lung and throat cancer, are all associated with dust inhalation. While the more serious risks are normally associated with exotic hardwoods, you should always take dust control seriously.

It is imperative that you use a good dust collection system. These systems operate like a vacuum, pulling air and dust particles into the system and trapping the particles in a filter. Dust collection systems come in all sizes and price ranges. Some are portable and can be moved easily. Others are larger and are incorporated into a complete workstation. There are also some large dust control machines that can be installed in the ceiling and operated remotely.

No dust control system will trap all of the dust particles generated while carving, so power carvers should wear a dust mask in addition to using a dust collection system. Whatever mask you choose, be sure it creates a good fit or seal between your face and the mask, has an exhaust valve, is made of face-friendly material, and has adjustable straps. Choose a comfortable mask and wear it when carving.

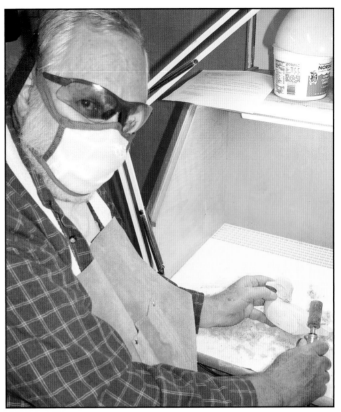

Safety equipment, such as a leather apron, dust mask, and safety glasses, should be used with a dust collection system.

Fire Hazard

Fire hazard is a danger related to dust, because it occurs where dust is not collected and disposed of. Uncontrolled and uncollected, airborne dust particles settle and build up on any exposed area or item. In a studio workshop, where all aspects of carving are dealt with, many situations can generate a spark.

A few worthy of consideration are:

- electrical motors and any heat- or spark-generating electrical appliances
- switches, outlets, and lightbulbs
- sparks generated from grinding metal when sharpening tools
- assembling metal armatures, bird legs, and supports with a soldering iron or torch
- heating elements
- torches used for soldering and bit cleaning
- improperly stored finishes
- spontaneous combustion from improperly discarded or uncared for finish rags, brushes, and wipes
- a tobacco smoker

Where smokers are concerned, "Don't worry, I'll be careful," isn't enough when a good portion of my livelihood can be affected by someone else's accident or carelessness. I have several highly visible "Absolutely No Smoking" signs prominently placed in my studios, and they have never been challenged.

Anywhere dust has settled, a fire path exists from the spark or flame source to anything combustible within the shop, and finally to the building itself. The answer to this type of hazard, of course, is to treat dust immediately as it is generated, direct it to a location for disposal, and not allow it to settle anywhere but where we want it. Even then, the shop should be inspected and cleaned whenever casual dust is observed, and dust from partially uncollected or uncollectible sources, like a table saw, should be cleaned.

Face and Eye Protection

When using any power equipment, always wear safety glasses to protect your eyes from flying debris. It is particularly important for power carving because the rotation of the bur is usually toward your face and therefore will propel particles in that same direction. Safety glasses or goggles, especially ones with side shields, will protect your eyes from dust and wood particles as well as particles of metal or material from the burs. Very rarely, the bur fractures during carving and pieces of material are thrown into the surrounding environment. Some carvers prefer real glass to plastic lenses because they find that glass doesn't have as much static electricity that holds wood dust to the lens the way plastic does. Some also prefer to wear a full face shield for some or all of their carving.

Body Protection

The greatest potential for injury occurs when large carbide or steel burs are used to remove wood quickly. The tool can slip or jump, especially when cutting into end grain. Carving with the grain is the safest way to use power and to minimize the potential for accidents. Clamping your project down when using large aggressive bits is also a good idea.

A leather apron protects power carvers and their clothes from cuts and tears. Avoid loose fitting clothes and tie back long hair. The use of a carving glove is not recommended because it can be dangerous if the fibers get caught in the equipment. Most newer micro motor carving equipment contains breakers or fuses that will stop the machine from rotating in such cases.

Creating power-carved sculptures like this one can produce flying debris, which the power carver must always be protected against.

A Guide to Power Carving Tools

You need a basic understanding of the tools before you can begin carving with power. The majority of power carvers use flexible shaft machines and micro motors. Both of these tools use a rotating bit or bur to remove wood. Flexible shaft machines have greater torque, but less speed, than micro motors. Specialized tools, such as angle grinders and air turbine machines, are also available for artists seeking specific results.

Flexible shaft machines have the power necessary for roughing out carvings as well as doing detail work. A flexible shaft machine is usually the first piece of equipment purchased by new carvers. The micro motor is primarily used as a detailer, although with a little patience it can be used to do rough shaping on small carvings. Many carvers invest in a micro motor as they gain experience. The higher speed of the micro motor produces cleaner cuts when carving fine detail.

It's impossible to say one model is better than another because it depends on what you want from your equipment. Think of it as buying a new car. Many people have brand preferences and each individual weighs features differently. Some people value gas mileage and efficiency, while others are looking for performance and durability.

Some tools make it easy to get started in power carving because of low initial cost. Other tools allow you more flexibility with a variety of available accessories. This article provides an overview of the equipment available and focuses on the models recommended for beginning carvers.

Basic Rotary Tools

The Dremel Moto-Tool came out in the 1930s, and it was touted as the Swiss Army knife of tools. These rotary tools are still marketed as useful for cutting, sanding, shaping, sharpening, grinding, and polishing. They also are a good way to start power carving. A Dremel or similar tool can be found in hardware stores, home improvement stores, and most larger retailers anywhere in the country, usually for less than $100.

These types of tools feature a high-speed motor with little torque, which means they depend on the speed of the tool to do the work. That makes them useful for light-duty carving, but you cannot expect them to remove a great deal of wood, even with a carbide bit.

The speed control, motor, and handpiece are combined into a single unit about the diameter of a drinking glass, so the overall size and bulk of the tool make it a challenge to carve for long periods of time. Some of these entry-level tools have a flexible shaft attachment with a handpiece that makes the tool more comfortable to use.

Foredom is a popular manufacturer of power carvers. The unit above is equipped with a flexible shaft, a handpiece, and a convenient foot pedal. Bits and burs, such as the ones pictured to the right, come in a variety of shapes, sizes, and materials.

In general, these entry-level models are a way to get started power carving, but most serious power carvers will quickly move on to larger flexible shaft tools to remove wood quickly and to micro motors to add the fine details. Then, these basic tools end up being used to cut off stuck bolts, sharpening lawnmowers, and other tasks you wouldn't want to do with more expensive tools.

Basic Rotary Tools At-a-Glance

Below are a few selected basic rotary tools. All are available for under $100, and many can be found right on the shelf at home improvement stores and large retailers. All of them can be ordered online from a variety of sources.

DREMEL 3000

- 32,000 rpm (max)
- 1.2 amp, 120 volt motor
- Weight: 20 oz

$$$

Dremel has less expensive units with less powerful motors, and more expensive units with more powerful motors and perks, such as tooless bit changes.

GYROS POWERPRO

- 32,000 rpm (max)
- 1.2 amp, 120 volt motor
- Comes with a flexible shaft attachment

$$

Gyros features an on-off switch separate from the speed control, so you can set your speed and not need to reset it each time you turn the tool off.

WEN 2305

- 30,000 rpm (max)
- 1 amp, 120 volt motor
- Comes with a flexible shaft attachment

$

The Wen 2305 is the least expensive and most widely available unit presented here.

PROXXON FBS 115/E

- 20,000 rpm (max)
- ⅛ hp motor
- Comes with a keyless chuck for bit shanks from ¹⁄₆₄" to ⅛" (.4mm to 3mm)

$$$

Proxxon's FBS 115/E is shaped to be more comfortable to hold for long periods of time. It features a slower but more powerful motor.

$ = $0–25
$$ = $26–50
$$$ = $50–100

Flexible Shaft Machines

The flexible shaft machine is the mainstay for power carving. Many power carvers use a flexible shaft machine for all of their power carving needs. We recommend you invest in a flexible shaft machine unless you plan to carve mainly small or miniature carvings. For small carvings less than 3" in height, a micro motor may fulfill your equipment needs.

The flexible shaft machine consists of an enclosed drive motor attached to a 36" or longer flexible shaft. A handpiece is attached to the shaft, which is covered by a polyethylene or neoprene sheath. Benchtop units are available, but the motor unit is about the size of a softball. Most carvers opt for the hanging units to free up space on their workbench. The rotational speed of the bur is controlled by a foot pedal or a dial.

The speed at which the shaft turns the bur is measured in revolutions per minute (rpm). The higher the rpm, the faster the bur will remove wood. Torque is the power behind the rpm. Flexible shaft machines range in power from $\frac{1}{15}$ horsepower to $\frac{1}{3}$ horsepower. Higher horsepower units will keep the machine from losing rpm while you are carving. If you plan to carve primarily hard wood, such as maple, choose a $\frac{1}{3}$ horsepower machine so the bur does not get bogged down in the dense wood.

Most machines have a forward and reverse setting. You want to keep the bur rotating toward you for maximum control. Reversing the direction allows you to carve with the grain when its direction changes, and it helps remove a stuck bur or drill bit. The reverse setting is also handy for directing dust away from you, toward the dust collector, while sanding.

Flexible Shaft Machine Handpieces

Handpieces come in a variety of sizes and shapes. Many manufacturer's handpieces are interchangeable with different brands of flexible shaft machines. The handpiece is the part of the tool you hold, and it should be comfortable to grip.

The handpiece connects to the flexible shaft on one end and secures the bit or bur in a collet on the other end. The bit or bur is the part that does the actual carving.

Most, but not all, handpieces accept varying size bits by changing the collet. Burs with large diameter shanks are primarily used for roughing out. Switch to a smaller collet or handpiece to accommodate burs with smaller shanks for shaping and detailing.

Some handpieces have a quick-change lever to expedite changing burs. However, most handpieces with this option will only accept a single shank size. Several manufacturers produce handpieces that utilize a geared three-jaw chuck. Similar to the three-jaw chuck on a drill press, these handpieces can hold any size shank accessory up to $\frac{5}{32}$" (4mm) diameter. This feature is quite useful for drill bits and other bits of nonstandard size.

As technology improves, handpieces are becoming more versatile. Some handpieces have an attachment that transforms them into mini-belt-sanders. Several manufacturers make a specialty handpiece that houses a reciprocating hammer-type mechanism. These handpieces accept a range of chisels used for power chisel or gouge carving. Reciprocating handpieces should only be used with the motor rotating forward.

A variety of handpieces, such as these units from Foredom, allow you to rough out your carving and add final details using the same flexible shaft machine.

At-a-Glance: Flexible Shaft Machines

Below you'll find an overview of the models we recommend for beginners from each manufacturer. Important factors to consider when shopping for a flexible shaft machine are reliability, availability of parts and service, speed, accessories, warranty, and cost.

FOREDOM 5240SR

- 18,000 rpm (max.)
- ⅛ hp motor
- Wide variety of accessories available

$

Foredom also makes a ⅓ hp TX series. Both SR and TX series offer benchtop and hanging units.

MASTER CARVER BASIC

- 26,000 rpm (max.)
- ⅓ hp motor
- Moderate variety of accessories available

$

Master Carver offers Pro and Ultra units that have identical motors, but include additional handpieces.

PFINGST CH

- 14,000 rpm (max.)
- ⅒ hp motor
- Limited accessories available

$

Discontinued ⅛ hp units manufactured by Pfingst may still be found at some retail locations.

WECHEER MODEL 340

- 26,000 rpm (max.)
- ¼ hp motor
- Moderate variety of accessories available

$

DREMEL 9100 FORTIFLEX

- 23,000 rpm (max.)
- ⅕ hp motor
- Three-jaw chuck accepts bit shafts up to ⁵⁄₃₂" (4mm) dia.

$

Dremel's interchangable hand-piece is compatible with other flexible shaft machines.

$ = $200–300
$$ = $300–500
$$$ = $500–1000

At-a-Glance: Micro Motor Machines

We have listed the model from each manufacturer that we believe is best suited for beginners. Many manufacturers offer a range of models.

Major factors to consider when shopping for a micro motor machine are reliability, diameter and weight of the handpiece, rpm, service and parts availability, warranty, and cost.

BRASSELER MIO

- 35,000 rpm (max.)
- Accommodates ³⁄₃₂" (2.5mm) shank bits. Optional collets include ¹⁄₁₆" (2mm) and ¹⁄₈" (3mm).

$ $ $

Brasseler produces four units marketed mainly to the dental industry.

FOREDOM 1070

- 38,000 rpm (max.)
- Accommodates ³⁄₃₂" (2.5mm) shank bits. Optional collets include ¹⁄₁₆" (2mm) and ¹⁄₈" (3mm).

$ $

Foredom provides a second model with a maximum rpm of 50,000.

$ = $200–300
$$ = $300–500
$$$ = $500–1000

Micro Motor Machines

Micro motor machines achieve speeds up to 50,000 rpm from a motor housed in the handpiece. Power is provided through a control box that includes an on/off switch, a dial or digital speed control, and a foot control/manual switch. The most expensive models have digital output. Although digital output is great for speed consistency, the cost may not justify the feature.

All of the machines outlined above include forward/reverse settings, overload protection, and a foot pedal. Some manufacturers only include one collet with their units. The additional collet may cost up to $60. Carvers seldom use a foot pedal to control the speed of the unit. Instead, most carvers set the speed manually so they can later repeat a specific speed to ensure the consistency of their carving and texturing.

Micro motor machines do not usually have high torque compared to flexible shaft machines and should not be used for roughing out large carvings. Micro motors operate at much higher speeds than flexible shaft machines. The handpiece on a micro motor may look heavier than the handpiece on a flexible shaft tool, but it is actually smaller and lighter, making micro motors easier to control. The connection between the handpiece and the power unit

on a micro motor machine is a lightweight electrical cord as opposed to the heavier connection of the flexible shaft machine. These features make it easier to use a micro motor for extended periods of time.

Micro motors are used primarily for detail carving and texturing. The majority of bird carvers use micro motor machines for the highly detailed texture characteristic of that style of carving. The higher speed of micro motors produces cleaner cuts.

The handpiece on a micro motor machine is connected to the power supply by a lightweight electrical cord.

GESSWEIN MARATHON HANDY 700

- 50,000 rpm (max.)
- Accommodates ⅛" (3mm) shank bits. Optional collets include ¹⁄₁₆" (2mm) and ³⁄₃₂" (2.5mm).

$ $ $

Gesswein offers three additional units ranging from 35,000 to 55,000 rpm.

MASTERCARVER MICRO-PRO

- 46,000 rpm (max.)
- Accommodates ⅛" (3mm) and ³⁄₃₂" (2.5mm) shank bits.

$

Mastercarver also produces a woodburner/micro motor combination unit.

NSK V-MAX

- 35,000 rpm (max.)
- Accommodates ³⁄₃₂" (2.5mm) shank bits. Optional ⅛" (3mm) collet.

$ $ $

NSK produces three additional units ranging from 35,000 to 50,000 rpm.

OPTIMA 2

- 45,000 rpm (max.)
- Accommodates ³⁄₃₂" (2.5mm) shank bits. Optional collets include ¹⁄₁₆" (2mm) and ⅛" (3mm).

$

PJL Enterprises also manufactures the Ultima, a combination woodburner/micro motor unit.

RAMPOWER 45

- 45,000 rpm (max.)
- Accommodates ³⁄₃₂" (2.5mm shank bits. Optional collets include ¹⁄₁₆" (2mm) and ⅛" (3mm).

$ $

Ram Products manufactures ten different units ranging from 20,000 to 45,000 rpm.

$ = $200–300
$$ = $300–500
$$$ = $500–1000

Air turbine units provide precision control for carving materials such as wood, egg shells, and glass.

Specialized Equipment

Flexible shaft and micro motor machines are the most common tools used by power woodcarvers. However, there are several self-contained handheld rotary tools including the models manufactured by Proxxon. There are also several types of specialized power tools employed by woodcarvers with specific needs.

Air Turbine Machines. Air turbine machines operate at up to 400,000 rpm and require the use of an air compressor. A foot pedal regulates the speed of the bur. Kits generally include a handpiece, regulator/filter, foot control pedal, hose, and lubricant. The handpiece accepts only ¹⁄₁₆"-diameter shaft burs. Only special friction grip burs rated at 350,000 to 400,000 rpm should be used in air turbine machines.

Air turbine units remove a small amount of material quickly and with great precision. Do not try to rough out a carving with an air turbine tool. In addition to wood, air turbine machines are used to carve egg shells, glass, ceramic, bone, antler, and metals. Air turbine machines are highly specialized tools and are generally purchased by carvers with specific carving needs, such as gunstocks.

Several manufacturers, such as Turbocarver, SMC, Powercrafter, and NSK, produce air turbine machines.

Angle Grinders. Angle grinders are used to remove a substantial quantity of wood quickly and efficiently using a large carbide disc or toothed chain (similar to a chainsaw). Several manufacturers, including Arbortech, Friction Coatings, and King Arthur Tools, manufacture these types of discs, which can be used in nearly any angle grinder. Most tool manufacturers, including Black & Decker, DeWalt, and Bosch, make angle grinders.

Using an angle grinder requires the use of both hands to hold the grinder, so the wood being carved must be clamped securely. It is important to wear safety glasses, a dust mask, leather gloves, leather apron, and other protective clothing when using an angle grinder. Chainsaw carvers frequently use an angle grinder to detail their carvings.

Carvers often use angle grinders to create detail in large chainsaw sculptures.

Choosing Your Power Carving Equipment

Whenever possible, test drive several different brands and models before making a purchase. Many stores and woodcarving shows provide consumers with the opportunity to try before buying. Pay attention to the comfort and weight of the handpiece. Try carving both hard and soft wood to determine the tool's ability to remove wood quickly. The equipment should not lose power even at low speed. Neither the handpiece nor the motor should vibrate or generate uncomfortable amounts of heat. Make sure the noise level is acceptable and determine how easy it is to remove and replace the handpiece and bits.

In addition to the overall quality of a tool, research the availability of technical support as well as parts and service. Does the manufacturer offer a toll-free number to call if your tool stops working? Is there a website you can visit to find tips and techniques for using and maintaining the tool? Be sure to think about what happens after the initial purchase.

Consider how much time you will be carving. Ask other carvers in your woodcarving club for their personal opinions or visit websites, such as the *Woodcarving Illustrated* forum *(www.woodcarvingillustrated/forum)*, where you can gather testimonials from a large group of power carvers. Keep in mind, though, that reviews from carvers are personal opinions and can vary in reliability.

In most cases, buy the best equipment you can afford. Generally, inexpensive tools wear out sooner and have to be replaced, therefore doubling your cost. Once you have decided on the unit you want to purchase, check with retailers for discounts or special package-deal pricing. The purchase of a power carving unit is an investment. With proper research, you can find a unit that will provide years of dependable performance, allowing you to concentrate on honing your carving skills.

CHECKLIST FOR POWER CARVING EQUIPMENT

- ☑ Comfortable handpiece
- ☑ Generates little vibration and heat
- ☑ Acceptable noise level
- ☑ Adequate technical support
- ☑ Availability of parts and service

Reciprocating power carvers add hammer-like action to traditional-edged tools.

Reciprocating Carvers. Reciprocating carvers are self-contained electronic units that use interchangeable chisels or gouges to remove wood. Generally, reciprocating carving units are held with both hands, so the wood being carved must be clamped. Reciprocating carvers allow you to produce a tooled surface, similar to the one produced by traditional hand tools, without as much effort. Arbortech, Flexcut, and Automach each have stand-alone reciprocating carvers. If you have a flexible shaft machine, you can purchase a reciprocating handpiece that simulates the function of a reciprocating carver on a small scale.

Woodburners. Woodburners usually consist of a power unit, a cord that attaches to a handpiece, and a tip or tips that fit the handpiece. The handpiece is often held like a pencil and used to augment the texturing and detail made with a power carving machine before any paint is applied. Bird carvers find woodburners particularly useful in their craft for creating lifelike feathers. There are a number of woodburner manufacturers, and each unit has different features to consider depending on your specific needs.

Woodburners usually consist of a power unit, a cord that attaches to a handpiece, and different types of tips. These units are often used to amplify texturing of hair, fur, and feathers.

Choosing the Right Bit

Just as there are a variety of power tools available from a variety of manufacturers, there are many bits offered in different shapes, sizes, and materials. Some materials are as hard as diamonds and some as fragile as ceramic. The bits go by names such as burs, cutters, carvers, stones, and disks. While the descriptions may seem baffling, all bits perform the same important operation: wood removal. Once you have the nomenclature mastered and acquire an understanding of bit composition, including the fact that "grit" is used here as it is when referring to sandpaper grade, the rest should be easy to follow.

To help you with making choices, first ask yourself the following questions:

- How fast do I want to remove wood?
- How much wood do I want to remove?
- How smooth do I want the finished surface to be?
- Which size and shape is best to use for a particular job?

Bit Types

One way bits are classified is by material. Different materials—carbide, ruby, diamond, steel, stone—cut with different levels of aggressiveness, have different grits within the materials, and are better at certain tasks than others.

Among the bits available are tungsten carbide burs. A distinguishing feature is points or "teeth" that are either randomly spaced or in perfect alignment. Two of the best-known brands are Kutzall and Typhoon. The Kutzall burs are offered with three colored grits: silver is coarse, gold is medium, and red is fine. Typhoon burs come in three

Diamond bits can be a good choice for fine detailing.

Carbide burs are aggressive cutters.

Fluted burs are designed to cut like rotary files.

Stump cutters remove wood much as fluted burs do, but more aggressively.

Texturing stones are made from different materials, including ceramic, and come in an assortment of textures.

grits but with some different colors: black is coarse, red is medium, and blue is fine.

A steel- or carbide-fluted bur, with rows of knife-like edges, cuts wood like a file. When the rows are parallel, the bur is described as "single cut." When rows cross each other, the bur is called "double cut." Both types are available in three grades—coarse, medium, and fine.

A variation of the fluted bur is the stump cutter, a bit that is sometimes described as a crosscut bur. Having rows of parallel, knife-like, serrated edges, the bur leaves a slightly ridged surface. Like their counterparts, these burs are also available in different grades of coarseness.

Ruby carvers and diamond bits get their names from the mineral deposits that are bonded to a steel shape and are available in various grits. Diamond bits are generally smaller in size than ruby carvers, but both types are very long lasting.

Made from silicon carbide, ceramic, or other abrasive materials, texturing stones are available in a variety of grits and are often identified by color. White stones are the finest grit and are most often used for fine detail texturing. Pink, green, and brown stones are coarser than white and are useful for fine detail shaping and smoothing. Ceramic blue stones are made from a hard material that should last a lifetime while providing a smooth finish.

If speed is your goal, tungsten carbide burs are the best choice. Unfortunately, the faster a bit cuts, the faster it gets loaded up with wood and stops cutting. Stump cutters also work well at taking away excess wood, but they are not as aggressive as their carbide cousins. However, some carvers often use fine stump cutters for detail shaping. For hogging off wood on a small scale, as well as for very fine detailing, ruby carvers and diamond bits may be a good choice.

To achieve a smooth finish, the finer the grit, the smoother the surface. For this reason, most texturing stones are ideal for smooth finishing, but finish is not dependent on bit grit alone. The other critical factor is the rotary tool's rpm. Follow this general rule: The coarser the grit, the slower the rpm; the finer the grit, the faster the rpm.

Bits, such as the ruby carvers shown here, come in many shapes.

Bit Profiles and Sizes

Bit shapes range from round to flame to needle. Choosing a shape that is best is often a matter of personal preference. A cylinder shape is excellent for smoothing a flat surface, while a round or ball-nose bit allows you to get into small spaces. Needle-shaped bits are invaluable for very tight areas and undercutting.

When it comes to choosing a size, select the largest bit that you are comfortable using. If you are hollowing a contoured area such as a spoon, for example, your obvious choice of shape is a ball-shaped bit. Using one that is only ⅛" (2mm) in diameter will leave many marks on the surface that need to be sanded out. A larger bit, ½" (1.3cm) or ¾" (1.9cm) in diameter, is a better choice because less sanding is required.

Bit Cleaners and Cleaning Materials

Because all bits become clogged at some time or another, you'll want to keep some materials on hand for bit cleaning. A propane torch is one method used to clear clogged carbide burs.

A stiff wire or bristle brush can be used alone for steel burs or after using the propane torch for carbide burs.

Oven cleaner followed by the stiff wire or bristle brush can also be used on carbide and steel burs, and ruby and diamond bits. Simply spray the bit head with oven cleaner, let it set for twenty to thirty minutes, and then brush it.

Neoprene (crepe) rubber blocks are useful for cleaning out ruby, diamond, and stone bits. Soaking these bits in equal parts of hot water and a commercial cleaner/degreaser concentrate also works very well if the bits haven't been extremely burned in.

A mineral block (wet stone) soaked in water works well for diamond bits. Simply rotate the bit slowly on the wetted material to clean it.

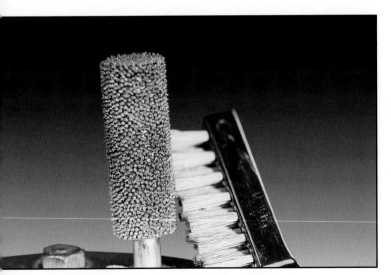

A stiff bristle brush removes debris from bits.

Bit Shapes

BALL:
- Use to create concave cuts and to hollow out areas
- Creates a cut similar to a U-gouge

CYLINDER:
- Use to cut flat areas, round edges, and make stop cuts and V-cuts
- Creates a cut similar to a knife or straight chisel
- Hold the tool at an angle and use the top corner to make V-cuts
- Smooth-end or safe-end bits are the most useful

FLAME:
- Use to make concave cuts and V-cuts, and to recess areas
- Creates a cut similar to a U-gouge when using its side and a V-tool when using the tip

PEAR:
- Use to round edges and create lumps and bumps when bird carving

BULL NOSE/BALL NOSE:
- Combines a ball with a cylinder
- Use to make concave cuts and hollow out areas using the top
- Use the side to cut flat areas and round edges
- Creates a cut similar to a U-gouge with the top and a knife cut with the side

LARGE TAPER:
- Use to round edges, make concave cuts, and access hard-to-reach areas

SMALL TAPER:
- Use to access hard-to-reach and angled areas
- Create feather barbules and hair

OVAL:
- Use to round edges, create lumps and bumps, and make concave cuts

INVERTED CONE:
- Use to make V-cuts for feather barbules and hair

DISC:
- Use to undercut feathers and make channel cuts
- Cut off thin pieces of unwanted wood

Carving Accessories

In addition to the power carving tools and their bits, the items in this section can help make your carving sessions easier and more enjoyable.

Light

Give yourself and your eyes every possible benefit when it comes to lighting. Insist on quantity and quality. I try to paint in natural light whenever possible because painting is the most demanding with respect to light and accuracy of color selection, blending, and application. Whenever natural light is not available or possible, I try to come as close to it with artificial lighting as I can. A combination of incandescent and fluorescent lighting has proven to be the most effective for me over the years. I have the studio ceiling, especially in the paint area, laid out so as to provide a ratio of two 100-watt clear incandescent bulbs for every 8' double run of fluorescent lights. If, for some reason, I need additional light in the immediate area I'm working, I use swing-arm lamps to augment the ceiling lights. No matter what, I let comfort be my guide.

Shadow Light

This is a harsh light, positioned so it falls across the work and casts a sharp shadow in or across any depression or cut made in the surface of the carving. Of greatest benefit when texturing hair, fur, or feathers, shadow light gives the carver an immediate report with respect to accuracy of register, depth, and positioning of texturing cuts. Though a shadow light is beneficial to texturing accuracy and providing an additional source of light, it can strain and tire the eyes with prolonged use.

Magnification

Magnifying visors of the type shown are available in various powers, giving optimum view at different focal lengths, so select a power that will give focused magnification at a distance most comfortable to you and where you like to hold your work. I try them first wherever they are sold near me, such as hardware stores, tool vendors, or woodcarving shows. If you use them as much as I have been forced to, you want to make a proper selection to begin with.

Handpiece Holder

A handpiece holder is essential for quick and convenient placing of the handpiece while the machine is winding down after being shut off. Without a holding device that allows the carver to safely put down the handpiece, he is left holding it while waiting for the rotation to stop completely. As often as we need to stop to sketch detail on the project, change bits, or just inspect work done, a handpiece hanger or holder is a must.

Flexible shaft handpieces require a secure upright holding device, such as a pronged cradle fixture, or bench mounted clips. Equipment clips work best for securing the handpiece to the side of the bench within easy reach. I have used ½" (13mm) PVC caps that were drilled and cut to size to hold the diameter of the upright handpiece, and then secured to the bench edge by flattening the back. They work beautifully (at about $0.24 each), but I have to remember to lift up, then out, and not pull straight away as with a clip.

The micro motor type handpieces require either a horizontal cradle or a tube type holder, which I prefer and consider the ultimate for giving the carver hands-off freedom. The handpiece can be placed, left in place, or removed while running without worry. The tube type holder can be made from any piece of PVC pipe that will encircle the handpiece and secure it in the position and angle desired by the carver.

Machine Hanger

The most common method to anchor a flexible shaft machine is to suspend it, as opposed to mounting it horizontally on a benchtop. Suspension affords far more freedom with respect to being tethered by the shaft. The hanger shown allows adjustment up or down, in or out, and at any point along the circumference of the hanger arm.

Stiff hanging devices support the machine best.

A stiff hanging device, such as the one shown, is preferred because hanging the machine on an S hook suspended on a cord or small chain will result in the machine twisting around every time it is turned on, due to the initial torque introduced when the machine is turned on.

A variety of customized homemade machine hangers can be easily made from materials found around the shop/studio, should the commercial hangers not fit your need (see page 28).

The simplest and most inexpensive movable hanger uses either metal or PVC pipe about 36" (91.44cm) long (I use ¾", or 19mm, outside-diameter metal conduit), a 3" (7.6cm) C-clamp, a threaded eyebolt with nut, and two ¼" (6mm) bolts, nuts, and lockwashers.

Bar clamps, telescoping aluminum channel, bent solid rod, and rigid ceiling hooks are but a few types of hangers that I have seen used.

A simple micro motor handpiece holder can be made from PVC.

This handpiece cradle keeps a handpiece from rolling around in the work area.

Handpiece Cradles

Before I begin to carve, I lay out all necessary equipment. For me, this requires setting up several handpieces, so I won't have to take time away from the project by changing bits back and forth. Until I found a way to corral those critters, at the slightest provocation, they chose to roll all over the work surface or onto the floor. So if you own one or more extra handpieces, find a convenient fixed location and mount however many cradles you need to hold extra handpieces. You will soon find you automatically reach in that direction when you want to change a handpiece. There are several ways to make horizontal handpiece cradles.

An inexpensive permanent method is to cut 6" (15.2cm) lengths of 1½" (3.8cm) PVC pipe in half lengthwise, sand a flat on the downward side, and screw the cradle to the benchtop with one or two countersunk screws. You can easily align as many PVC cradles as needed at very little cost.

Another inexpensive method to contain more than one idle handpiece requires a block of wood with at least 5" (12.7cm) width and a minimum 2" (5.1cm) thickness. The block is turned on its edge, and 1¼" (3.2cm) holes are drilled completely through it from side to side. Drill as many holes as you have handpieces, remembering that each hole will serve two handpieces. Cut the block, still on edge, along a centerline through the holes from end to end. The result yields two grooved blocks that nicely hold and provide easy access to handpieces as they are used and replaced.

Handpiece cradles can also be easily made from PVC.

Bit Stand

Even with a few bits required to accomplish the different aspects of a carving, a secure organized (usually upright) bit stand is helpful so that at a glance, a needed bit can be located, easily accessed, and replaced. It is frustrating having to stop and waste time to look for a misplaced bit. I have seen bit stands made from wood, plastic, and steel, with flat, terraced, circular, sloped, and even ball-shaped presentation surfaces. Every one has served purpose and pocketbook, depending on a user preference and choice.

This wooden bit stand rotates.

A nice bit stand can be made from wood.

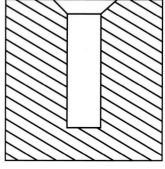

Slightly countersinking the existing hole gives an area for the bit end to fall into.

The most important aspect of any bit stand is not size, shape, or capacity, but ease of replacement and retrieval of bits. Simple straight drilled holes require more effort when replacing a bit (especially the smaller bits) among other bits, because the opening is so small. However, a hole with a "lead" for the end of the bit shank, will allow the bit end to follow into the lead and slide into the hole without any maneuvering around to find the hole. Making a hole lead requires no more than slightly countersinking the existing hole to provide an extra area for the bit end to fall into.

I prefer homemade wooden bit stands and accessory trays above all, because I can choose different woods for beautiful grain patterns, I have greater versatility with how I arrange what I want to place on the stand or tray, and I can more easily drill the bit holes to size and arrangement. If I decide to change the arrangement, wood allows me to more easily change the configuration than does metal or plastic.

To date, preference lies with a bit stand that rotates on a small Lazy Susan fixture with a square base that has sections for chuck wrenches, collets, and shaping/cleaning blocks.

Accessory Tray

Beyond machines and bits, I consider a well-organized, easily accessible, and conveniently placed (or transported) accessory tray an absolute necessity. Organized accommodation for bits and other accessories such as chuck wrenches, shaping stones, cleaning blocks, and whatever else we feel a need for, is a requirement for continuous and timesaving carving. My work surface gets cluttered enough without having to filter through several layers of debris in search of my favorite flame-shaped ruby carver.

Most accessory trays include a bit stand, handpiece cradle(s), compartments for chuck wrenches, collets, and/or corrals for shaping and cleaning block. No matter what size, shape, or layout, make sure the accessory tray serves you.

Sanding Mandrel

The homemade sanding mandrel is a neat idea I picked up from a carving seminar I was giving in Florida. I saw it in several of the student bit stands and found it was homemade and great for use on larger pieces such as duck bodies and heads. I was given one and have been using and making my own ever since.

The mandrel can be obtained from a carving vendor, or from a flea market as the ones shown here were. It has a ¼" (6mm) shaft, and a ¾" (1.9cm) rubber expanding bushing used to hold a great variety of abrasive and polishing sleeves.

The expanding consists of a fairly hard rubber bushing that fits around the shaft of the mandrel and expands as the nut is tightened upward on the reverse threaded portion of the mandrel shaft.

The homemade part of this bit consists of a foam rubber sleeve made from a short length of pipe insulation to which a size matching sleeve of sandpaper has been affixed, using double-backed carpet tape between insulation and sandpaper, and rubber contact cement as an adhesive for the sandpaper seam. Note: Make sure any overlap is lapped so that the trailing edge is away from the rotation of the machine and not into it.

The entire sanding sleeve assembly slides over the rubber mandrel bushing, and the nut is tightened just enough to firmly hold the sanding sleeve in place.

An accessory tray keeps all of your tools organized and close at hand.

A homemade sanding mandrel can be great for sanding larger pieces.

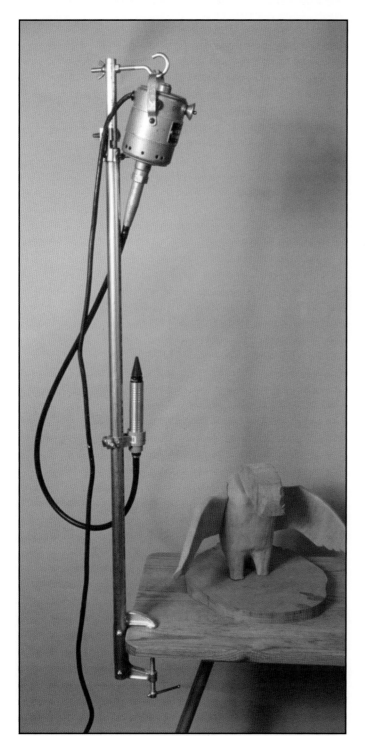

Collapsible Telescoping Rod

By Lynn Diel

After purchasing a flexible shaft tool, I realized I would have to hang it before I could use it, which led to an engineering challenge.

For my needs, I wanted the hanger to be adjustable so that I could use it while standing or sitting. In addition, I wanted the rod to be as compact as possible to make it portable.

After scrounging around my junk boxes, I found the leg from a discarded camera tripod. It looked like it would have possibilities. After assembling the device, I attached it to my workbench, placed my flexible shaft tool on the hanger, and put it to use. Adjustment was easy because I was able to change the height by releasing one of the fasteners for the leg.

When Christmas came around, I received another flexible shaft tool. I now had two with only one hanger. I added a second hanger to the tripod leg, but I soon found I needed a stronger support. That led to my latest invention.

When designing a tool or accessory, I strive to build something that does not require a full woodworking or machine shop. This has led to strange looks from sales staff and others as I walk around hardware stores looking for parts that seem to have no logical association with my latest design.

After deciding that the major components for my collapsible telescoping rod would be conduit, I purchased 36" (91.44cm) sections of ½" (1.3cm)- and ¾" (1.9cm)-diameter pipe, which made for a simple assembly. But the locking mechanism proved to be the most challenging part of the project.

Figure 1. Base Assembly

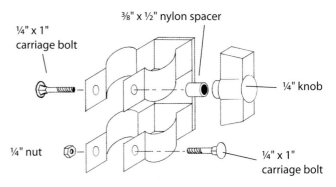

Figure 2. Threaded Knob Assembly

Construction

The ½" by 2" (1.3cm by 5.1cm) flat steel provides the bridge that holds the two conduit holders together. Two ³⁄₁₆" (5mm) carriage bolts and nuts hold the flat steel to the two conduit clamps. After putting the base assembly together (see **Figure 1**), the next step is to make the threaded knob assembly. Use carriage bolts so that the threaded knob and holding nut can be attached (see **Figure 2**). Secure the base assembly to the ¾" (1.9cm) conduit by tightening the ¼" (6mm) nut onto the ¾" (1.9cm) conduit clamp. The base assembly on pipe is complete (see **Figure 3**).

Next, construct a slider assembly that fastens to the ½" (1.3cm) conduit, allowing it to slide inside the ¾" (1.9cm) conduit. The slider consists of a ¾" (1.9cm)-diameter by 2" (5.1cm)-long dowel. It allows the conduit to slide up and down without rattling or excessive play. Attach the dowel to the ½" (1.3cm) conduit with epoxy glue. An alternative is to drill a small hole in the conduit and insert a nail or screw to hold the dowel in place (see **Figure 4**).

For the hook assembly, drill a ⁵⁄₁₆" (8mm)-diameter hole 1" (2.5cm) from the top of the ½" (1.3cm) conduit, insert the ¼" (6mm)-diameter by 6" (15.2cm)-long hook into the pipe, and tighten the two nuts (see **Figure 5**). If you want two hooks, drill a second ⁵⁄₁₆" (8mm)-diameter hole 1" (2.5cm) below the first one.

Next, slide the ½" (1.3cm) conduit past the ½" (1.3cm) conduit clamp and into the ¾" (1.9cm) conduit. The telescoping rod assembly is complete (see **Figure 6**). Adjusting the rod is simple. Loosen the threaded knob and slide the bar up or down. Then, tighten the knob to lock the rod in place.

**Figure 3.
Base Assembly on Pipe**

½" conduit

¾" x 2" dowel

Attach dowel to conduit with glue or small nail

Trim dowel to fit into the ½" conduit

¾" conduit

Figure 4. Slider Assembly

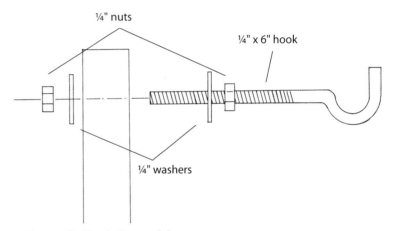

¼" nuts

¼" x 6" hook

¼" washers

Figure 5. Hook Assembly

**Figure 6.
Telescoping Rod
Assembly**

¾" x 2" dowel rod

¼" locking nuts

¼" x 1½" bolts

C-clamp

**Figure 7.
Clamp Assembly**

add weight to stabilize the platform

power connector and cord

**Figure 8.
Simple Base on Wheels**

plastic 5-gallon bucket filled with sand for weight

**Figure 9.
Weighted Bucket on Wheels**

**Figure 10.
Cabinet on Wheels**

Storage

Front

Dust collection back

Filter

Lap tray collector

Dryer hose

Figure 11. Dust Collector on Wheels

To make the clamp assembly, which allows the rod to be secured to a table, drill two ⁵⁄₁₆" (8mm)-diameter holes into a C-clamp and two matching holes into the ¾" (1.9cm) conduit (see **Figure** 7). Use two ¼" by 1½" (6mm by 3.8cm) bolts and locking nuts to secure the conduit to the C-clamp. Note: Be careful not to overtighten the nuts, which could bend the conduit.

Options

By using longer sections of conduit, a simple base on wheels can be constructed. An outlet box and power cord is incorporated into the pipe and a sandbag can be placed on the base for stability (see **Figure 8**).

An alternative is filling a five-gallon container with sand to create a weighted bucket on wheels (see **Figure 9**). A board will have to be placed on the bottom of the bucket to hold the bottom end of the conduit in place.

As I began to use my flexible shaft tool, it became evident that I would need storage for the accessories. I modified the original design to make a cabinet on wheels (see **Figure 10**) that holds bits and other components.

After finding that flexible shaft tools generate quite a lot of dust, I modified my cabinet to accommodate a small squirrel-cage fan and filter. When attached to a hose and lap tray, I have a dust collector on wheels (see **Figure 11**).

Like most carvers, I never have too many drawers for storage. I modified my cabinet on wheels by doubling its height and adding additional drawers. I also changed the holder on top to give me a cabinet with two rods (see **Figure 12**).

**Figure 12.
Cabinet with Two Rods**

Estimated Cost

The prices listed are what I paid at a local hardware chain store to build the basic collapsible telescoping rod with C-clamp.

Quantity	Description	Cost ($)
2	³⁄₁₆" x ½" (5mm x 1.3cm) carriage bolts	0.16
2	³⁄₁₆" (5mm) locking nuts	0.32
1	½" x 2" (1.3cm x 5.1cm) flat steel	0.49
1	½" (1.3cm) electrical conduit clamp	0.75
1	¾" (1.9cm) electrical conduit clamp	0.75
1	⅜" x ½" (1cm x 1.3cm) nylon spacer	0.15
2	¼" x 1" (6mm x 2.5cm) carriage bolts	0.18
1	¼" (6mm) nut	0.08
1	¼" (6mm) threaded tee knob	1.29
1	½" x 36" (1.3cm x 91.44cm) electrical conduit	0.87
1	¾" x 36" (1.9cm x 91.44cm) electrical conduit	1.77
1	¾" x 2" (1.9cm x 5.1cm) dowel rod	0.05
1	¼" x 6" (6mm x 15.2cm) hanger bolt	1.49
2	¼" (6mm) washers	0.04
2	¼" (6mm) nuts	0.08
1	C-clamp	3.49
2	¼" x 1½" (6mm x 3.8cm) bolts	0.18
2	¼" (6mm) locking nuts	0.38
	Total	$12.52

Power Carving Techniques

Whether you're just starting out in power carving or you're looking to hone your texturing skills, this section has tips from the experts to help you get the results you want.

Power Carving Bits, by Jack Kochan, page 38.

The Basics of Power Carving

By Frank Russell

Carving:

"The process of defining and refining shape by an orderly sequence of artistic cutting."

Reference Materials

Reference materials are the most important aspect to any carving—especially for a first-time subject. I constantly admonish my students to surround themselves with every photo, study skin/mount, artist's rendition, and descriptive material they can find before beginning a carving. References must be used through the entirety of the carving. "You can't carve what you don't know!"

Wasting

Wasting refers to the removal of unwanted stock. A colloquialism for wasting is "hogging," which is the removal of large amounts of wood usually in a quicker and more random manner than one would use when finish or detail carving.

Roughing

A term that refers to bringing the carving to a recognizable stage. Rough shaped denotes a general form but one without detail, texture, or refinement.

Relieving

Relieving is the act of raising a surface or shape away from a background. For example, ears are relieved from the sides of the head, and a curl is relieved from the hair mass.

Shaping

Shaping gives refined form to a general or roughed shape. The form becomes more recognizable at this point.

Detailing

Detailing is giving finished detail to refined shape. The detailed shape of a head, such as in the photo above, has details as required by the refined shapes—the mouth has lips, the eyes have irises and lids, the nose has nostrils, any hair mass is defined with curls, separations, etc.

Texturing

Texturing refers to final and finishing refinement that gives character and reality to the carving. Texturing of hair, see the photo above, gives greater depth and realism to the head; wrinkles and creases on the head represent age or aging; transitional contours such as temples, cheeks, cheekbones, and chin can indicate everything from nationality to physical condition.

Using the Handpiece

For the beginning power carver, learning to control the handpiece is paramount.

Understanding the reason why a handpiece rotates in the direction it does is the first step to using it properly.

The handpiece rotation is toward the carver by necessity—giving several advantages to the user. First, the handpiece is easier to control with the rotation toward the carver, in that the power and torque of the handpiece can effortlessly be brought under sustained control. This control is usually exerted by using the thumb as an anchor point, then drawing the handpiece in the general direction of the thumb, in the same manner a knife is used (see above).

Second, the direction of the cut is observable because the bit cuts into the stock on the carver's side of the rotation, allowing him to view, and therefore control, depth of cut as well as amount of stock removed.

If the rotation runs away from the carver, he fights against the natural closing action of the hand by either having to open away and possibly lose control, or he has to follow the cutting stroke with his entire forearm, losing control of cut and rotation as it runs away or into the stock.

I am often asked why the reverse is necessary on a machine, and my response is that for almost all applications it isn't necessary—to a right-handed carver. For the left-handed carver, a reversible machine is a must, to my way of thinking, because it gives him/her all the advantages mentioned above that are given to the right hander with forward rotation.

Whether right- or left-handed, a habit that must be mastered and continuously used, is that of establishing an anchor or pivotal control point between the carving and the bit. Anchoring with either the thumb or little finger (depending on the cut) provides steadiness and stability to the cut that allows control.

If a wasting or shaping stroke is being executed with a large handpiece and requires a heavy "hogging" cut, the thumb must be anchored and so placed as to exercise strength and control over the cut (see **Figure 1**). If only the bit makes contact with the carving, and the whole hand is closed around the handpiece, the control and pivotal point goes clear out to the carver's elbow.

If texturing or detail shaping with the handpiece held like a pencil, the little finger must maintain contact with the carving as the pivotal or control point, or the exactness required for this type of cut is lost because the control point moves to the wrist or in some cases, to the elbow (see **Figure 2**).

There are some wasting strokes where no great amount of control is needed, and the anchor point can be lifted; except for this, precise carving can only be obtained by establishing and maintaining an anchor point (see **Figure 3**).

Optional Knives and Chisels

I always keep my hand tools within easy reach because no matter how much I love power carving—its speed, economy of effort, and its applications—there are still those few times when it is just as quick and easy to use an appropriate knife or chisel.

If I want to clean out the corner of an eye, for example, there are times when a knife will serve as well and is quicker than changing a bit. When I checker gunstocks with power, there are tight areas that the power bit will leave me to manually point up and/or finish out to an edge.

Lastly, and the biggest reason I will never be without my hand tools, is that they serve me during some wonderful times of peace and quiet. When I am in the woods or on a beach, a higher power always allows me to find a piece of driftwood or fallen branch to keep my hands busy. As I carve a face or a figure, nature works its magic around me, and my mind sorts and settles the complexities of my life.

Figure 1 - The thumb acts as an anchor point for power strokes (palm grip)...

Figure 2 - ...and the little finger acts as an anchor point for detailing and texturing (pen grip).

Figure 3 - Control is lost or reduced without an anchor point.

Be a Pro: Safety Tips

By Jack Kochan

A homemade hanger for a flexible shaft machine consists of a pipe clamp fixture, pipe and shelf bracket with a J hook end. Note that the power cord is tied back so that it does not interfere with the power carving.

On the Safe Side

Maintaining a flexible shaft machine, or any other power carving tool, is necessary to protect your investment. Still, more may be required when working with power tools. Safety is the number one issue that comes up constantly when writing or talking about woodcarving, and it cannot be ignored here. Here are some tips I employ in my shop.

Be careful of overconfidence. Many of the rotating accessories available to power carvers have the ability to remove flesh as well as wood. Most of the hand-gouging accidents I hear about are the result of feeling overly comfortable removing wood. The tendency is to push the limits of the rotary tool. Don't try to take away too much wood in too short a time or force the bit into the wood so that it slips.

Know when to clamp your project. When using large and aggressive carbide bits, such as those used to rough out, you should clamp your piece to your work bench. It is very easy to apply too much pressure with the bit, and that is when accidents happen—however, clamping will save you a lot of pain. If clamping isn't possible, then a heavy leather welding glove is recommended. Do not substitute a standard carving or Kevlar glove—just as long hair will tangle around a moving bit, so will these gloves, often causing more harm than good.

Protect yourself from wood dust. All wood dust is potentially hazardous to your health. Use a dust collector when power carving. It can be as simple as a floor fan with a pleated filter taped to the backside. If that proves to be impractical or too expensive, then a dust mask is mandatory. Paper masks are available at hardware stores and home centers, but they don't afford maximum protection.

Wear safety glasses and an apron. Safety glasses will shield your eyes from flying chips, dust, and even a small piece of a bit that can break loose. Because loose clothing often poses a hazard due to the rotating bit, don a leather apron. And if you have long hair, make sure to tie it back.

Avoid clutter. Work surfaces piled with tools and accessories distract you from knowing where that rotating bit is at all times. Knock something off your worktable or bench, and the tendency is to grab it with the hand holding the power tool's handpiece and rotating bit.

Putting Your Foot Down

A simple on/off foot switch that controls a flexible shaft machine or many other power tools in your shop is readily available and costs about $15. To operate, plug the power tool into the foot switch, which plugs into an electrical outlet. A foot switch is available for flexible shaft machines to control the rpm, making it a variable speed accessory as well. The same principle runs many sewing machines. How fast your machine operates depends on how much pressure you apply to the foot pedal.

Power Carving Hang Ups

Micro motor tools, air turbine machines, and reciprocating carvers do not need to be mounted. Thanks to the design of the flexible shaft tool, it does need to be made stationary on a benchtop or suspended from above. Solutions to mounting the flexible shaft tool include a simple hook in the ceiling; an intravenous stand; and even an overhead pipe with a mountain climber's carabiner that allows the tool to move freely across the length of the pipe. Side-mounting cradles are commercially available that hold the canister in place and keep it from rolling off the work surface. Also available are stands that clamp to the workbench and hold the canister on a hanger.

My poor man's solution to having a vertical hanger—one that cost me under $20 in materials from a home improvement center—consists of a pipe clamp fixture, a 3' (91.44cm) length of pipe, and a shelf bracket with a J-hook at the end. The commercial models usually have a safety pin that prevents the motor canister from coming off the hanger, so a hole can be drilled into the bracket and a simple cotter pin inserted. See the Collapsible Telescoping Rod on page 28 for another option.

Power Carving Bits

Photographs by Carl Shuman

Power carving gives a carver the speed and control to complete a carving quickly and cleanly. The following photos serve as a brief introduction to the tools, grips, and cuts used in power carving.

Flexible shaft, ball-nosed cylinder-shaped carbide cutter

1 ***Rough in.*** Flexible shaft machines provide the necessary torque and power to complete the first step in power carving—roughing in. Here, I am using a carbide cutter on a flexible shaft machine to remove wood from the neck joint of this decoy. I am using an overhand grip, curling my fingers over the top of the tool's handle. My thumb acts as a brace against the wood, and cuts are made toward the thumb.

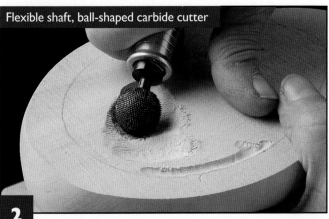

Flexible shaft, ball-shaped carbide cutter

2 ***Remove large amounts of wood.*** The same overhand grip is used for any coarse work on any area of a carving. Here, I am using a large ball-shaped carbide cutter to hollow out the inside of a decoy. Cutters are often color-coded to indicate different degrees of coarseness. For this one, a Typhoon, red indicates a coarser cut than blue.

Micro motor, medium-grit cylinder-shaped carbide cutter

3 ***Do any light roughing and shaping.*** In this photo, I am using a micro motor, which are commonly used for light roughing in and shaping. Smaller coarse cutters are available for smaller areas and projects. Because I am still roughing out wood, I continue to hold the tool with an overhand grip. Here, I am roughing in the head of this baby bird with a medium-grit cylinder-shaped carbide cutter.

Micro motor, medium-grit cylinder-shaped carbide cutter

4 ***Continue light roughing.*** Here, I move on to rough out the bird's shoulder. Notice in all of these pictures that my thumb is out of the direct path of the tool. Use carefully controlled, smooth strokes, and don't be tempted to remove too much wood at once. Always move the tool, not the wood.

Micro motor, tapered stump cutter

5 ***Smooth and shape.*** Both micro motors and flexible shaft machines work well for smoothing and shaping. I use the micro motor, but notice how my grip has changed. Holding the tool as I would hold a pencil gives me greater control over the smaller, more precise movements used in this stage. My little finger acts as a pivot and support point.

Micro motor, ball-shaped stump cutter

7 ***Make holes and indentations.*** Depending on how you hold your tool, many bits and burs will give you the same result. I find that hollowing out the eye of a bird or other animal is easy with a ball-shaped stump cutter. Note that this cutter does not make the actual hole for the eye, but just the indentation. This can be followed by a cylinder-shaped cutter to complete the hole.

Micro motor, cylinder-shaped blue stone

9 ***Make flat cuts and square edges.*** Cylinder-shaped stones are perfect for flat cuts that require a square edge. I find them especially useful here on the wing feathers of the avocet. Each feather will have a flat, sloping surface that appears to be tucked under the previous feathers. The square edge of the cylinder adds to this appearance. This shape also works well for animal hooves and the cuffs on shirt sleeves.

Micro motor, flame-tipped blue stone

6 ***Make undercuts.*** A variety of bits and burs are available. Matching a particular bit to the area you are working will make the tool more efficient. Here, I am using a flame-tipped blue stone to undercut the wing. I am using the side of the stone, not the very point. The flame shape of the stone allows me to cut a shallow indentation with a narrow groove.

Micro motor, small round blue stone

8 ***Lay out details.*** A small round blue stone works well to lay out individual feathers. Here, I am working on an avocet. I move the stone carefully around the penciled-in edge of the feather in one smooth motion. My little finger acts as a pivot point and helps keep the tool steady. I retrace the cut to make it deeper.

Micro motor, needle-point diamond

10 ***Carve deep undercuts.*** Occasionally, some areas of a carving need to be deeply undercut. On the avocet, I need to undercut the areas where the tail feathers overlap. A needle-point diamond works extremely well here. Note again that I am not using the very tip of the point, but the side.

11 **Round a carving.** Here, I am using a ruby to round over the shoulder. Rubies are not as hard as diamonds, but depending on their grit, they can give a smoother cut. The tapered shape of this bit allows me to make a slight indentation at the shoulder.

Micro motor, round-nosed tapered ruby

Flexible shaft, pointed white stone

13 **Continue defining.** A pointed white stone helps me define the baby bird's mouth. Again, avoid using the very point of the stone; focus on laying the tool on its side and using the surface close to the tip. Note that the tip of this stone is black. A little applied pencil lead gives an even smoother cut.

Air turbine, tapered cone-shaped white stone

15 **Finish texturing.** The side of this very small tapered cone will leave behind fine texturing marks on the cheek feathers. Pencil lead applied to the surface of the stone will give it a smoother cut.

Flexible shaft, tapered cylinder-shaped white stone

12 **Texture a carving.** Flexible shaft machines or air turbines are good choices for this next stage of power carving—texturing. Texturing requires very controlled movements, so my grip on the tool hasn't changed. I often choose softer stones over diamonds and rubies for fine detailing.

Air turbine, inverted cone-shaped white stone

14 **Detail.** An air turbine runs at much higher rpm than a micro motor or a flexible shaft and is excellent for detail work. The tan marks on the surface of this bird are the result of the friction from the high rpm. They are easily covered during painting and finishing. An inverted cone is often used to texture feathers, animal fur, or human hair.

CHANGING COLLETS **TIP**

The collet, shown here being removed from the end of a flexible shaft handpiece, can be changed to accept different-sized bits.

When the new collet is in place, the retaining collar is replaced, a bit is inserted, and the collar is tightened with the wrench. The locking pin is then removed and the tool is ready for use.

Reshaping Texturing Stones

Some carvers may find it beneficial, and even economical, to shape their own texturing stones. Jack Kochan buys cylinder-shaped texturing stones by the dozen and uses a diamond hone to create his own custom shapes.

"This way I can get shapes that are not available from the manufacturers," Jack says. "I can also avoid purchasing sets of stones. I always find several shapes in there that I never use and some that I use all the time."

Texturing stones are made from an abrasive material that is formed and molded to a cylindrical shaft. The shaft protrudes approximately one-fourth to one-third of the way into the stone. Because the material is not just embedded on the surface of the metal shaft (like ruby or diamond stones), any texturing stone can be honed to any shape—inverted cones, tapers, points, etc.

Any color stone can be reshaped as well—from the finer white stones to the coarser pink stones. To keep the "coarseness" of the original stone, Jack suggests choosing a diamond hone with the same abrasive qualities.

A cylinder-shaped white texturing stone in a flexible shaft handpiece is applied to a diamond hone to change its shape.

Cylinder-shaped stones can be re-shaped to tapers, points, inverted cones, and just about any custom shape needed to complete a carving project.

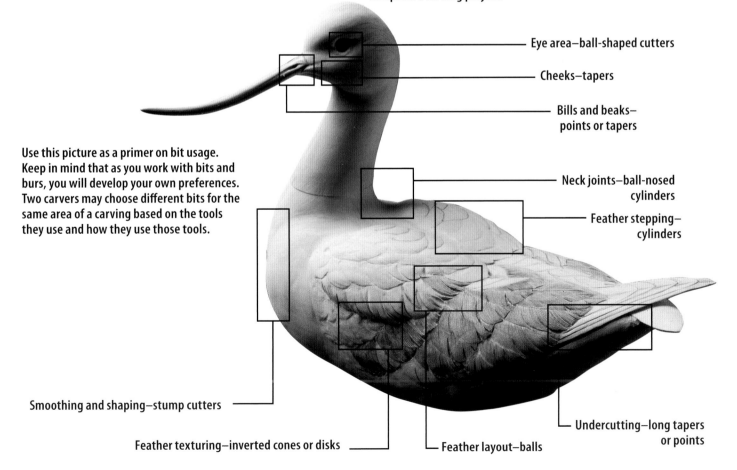

Eye area—ball-shaped cutters

Cheeks—tapers

Bills and beaks—points or tapers

Neck joints—ball-nosed cylinders

Feather stepping—cylinders

Use this picture as a primer on bit usage. Keep in mind that as you work with bits and burs, you will develop your own preferences. Two carvers may choose different bits for the same area of a carving based on the tools they use and how they use those tools.

Smoothing and shaping—stump cutters

Feather texturing—inverted cones or disks

Feather layout—balls

Undercutting—long tapers or points

Texturing Feathers

By Frank Russell

Understanding Feathers

Before you can skillfully replicate feathers on a carving, you must first understand something about them. Knowing a bit about the different types and functions of feathers found on a bird is essential to creating a realistic and accurate woodcarving. Knowing how to create feathers as a whole, in part, and as a group is a necessity to creating the pleasing effect that they produce on a carving. The higher the degree of skill you attain in this area, the greater the ease, and the greater the rewards.

Remember: You cannot carve what you don't know. Learn as much as you can about feathers as a subject. As you immerse yourself in the references required (mounts, study skins, photos, drawings) to carve a bird, you will find that this knowledge of feathers will serve you well. Ultimately, knowledge of feathers will give you a greater understanding of the bird you are carving and reduce the effort you put forth toward the completion of a fine bird carving.

Feather Facts

The main composition of a feather is keratin. Keratin is described as minuscule fibrils and larger filaments held together by an amorphous protein matrix substance. I asked a chemist friend of mine for a description of keratin in a language I could understand, and he said, it's pretty much protein . . . that's why chickens will eat feathers. Sounds like chemical talk to me.

Once a feather fully matures, its supply of blood is terminated and, similar to human hair, has no feeling.

On most birds, feathers do not cover the entire body, but are usually grouped into eight or more major groups called feather tracts. The tract areas are the tail, upper legs, leading and trailing wing edges, along the back, both sides of the underbody, and the head. The areas between these feather tracts are bare on most birds—although some birds, such as penguins, are solidly covered without these bare spaces between the tracts. Within these tracts are definable feather groups that will be described later.

There is nothing that a bird's body can do to repair broken feathers, so it must wait until a broken or old feather molts (falls off) and a new one replaces it. I have seen major flight feathers (especially primary and tail feathers) repaired by ornithologists and vets by splicing and gluing the hollow center shaft within with everything from wire to bamboo skewers.

Types of Feathers

Flight feathers are the feathers that sustain flight and maneuverability. They are the strongest feathers, and although structurally rigid, are quite flexible in length and within movement of the group. They are the main feathers found in the wings and the tail. Most of the time they are textured by woodburning owing to the desired harder, stiffer appearance that can be gained by burning as opposed to stone texturing.

Contour feathers are fan or elongated fan-shaped feathers that cover the bird's outer body. These feathers lie in such a way as to give the body a softer, rounded appearance. For this reason, many woodcarvers prefer to grind texture them with a rotary stone bit.

Down feathers lie hidden beneath contour feathers and function to insulate the bird from heat or cold. Where applicable, some advanced carvers will show just a touch of down squeezing out from beneath contour feathers in such a manner as to indicate that a feather is missing and a bit of the down has become exposed. This is done sparingly, usually no more than five or six places on an entire bird, and then only in areas known for down, such as the breast or underbelly areas.

Filoplume feathers are extremely small feathers, always hidden from view, that look like hair and are found in tufts around and at the base of certain contour feathers.

Bristle is a feather that grows almost exclusively on a bird's head and neck (see **Figure 1**). Rictal bristles grow on either side of a bird's mouth and are more pronounced on some birds than others.

Feather Functions

The feathers on a bird have four primary functions: to maintain flight, to insulate, to waterproof, and to attract. Additionally, feathers function as camouflage on some species of birds, such as the ruffed grouse, woodcock, and many female species of ducks, songbirds, and shorebirds. The camouflage is used not only to shield a nesting female, but also to guard against predators. On many species of male birds, the feather colors function in just the opposite manner, in that they are used to attract and defend. Feathers are used to attract a female during the mating and bonding period, while at the same time, their brightness is used to repel would-be suitors. Feather brilliance is also used by the male to attract and draw a predator away from the nesting site.

Rictal Bristles

Figure 1
Carefully observe these feathers as you carve your bird, and decide not only how prominent they are, but also, on some, how you will accomplish putting them on. Most of the time they are relieved with a fine bit, then accentuated with a woodburner (on hawks, owls, eagles). On some songbirds, it is sufficient just to paint them on with a very fine pointed brush.

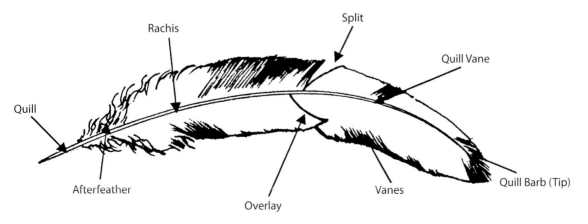

Figure 2 - Feather Nomenclature

Feather Structure

It is important to know that the outside shape of any bird's body is greatly changed by the feathers that lie within specified groups. The shape of each group (in most cases) must be determined before individual feathers can be laid out, detailed, and textured. Familiarize yourself with the most prominent wing and body feather groups and how they are shaped and flow on a particular bird.

The main stem of the feather is called the quill at its tip, rachis or shaft, vane, and barb beginning at the tip that attaches to the skin at the feather follicle. It progresses to the tip that the stiff barb end of the quill runs through (see **Figure 2** and **Figure 3**).

Running out from this main stem are parallel interlocked rays or barbs, and along each barb are even rows of interlocked, smaller raylike barbules, on which are rows of minuscule hooks or barbecels; these interlock to hold the barbs together in a network all the way around the quill. When you see a bird preening, it is realigning and interlocking all of the parts of the feather network. This network gives the feather shape and strength, and when stacked or layered against other feathers, provides enough strength to sustain the weight of the bird in flight. To gain a better understanding of this structure, fan the tail of a bird and note how the quill of each feather is positioned so as to add strength to the tail as a whole. First, you will note the tail of any bird is divided into two even sections, and each

Upper

Lower

Figure 4 - Typically Paired Tail Feathers

Figure 3 - Magnified Feather Detail

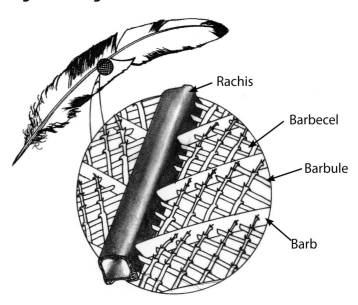

Rachis

Barbecel

Barbule

Barb

feather in one section will have a mate or counterpart in the opposite section. The result? Every bird's tail has an even number of feathers, with the vast majority having 12 for a feather count (see **Figure 4**). Most hummingbirds, swifts, and cuckoos have ten tail feathers, while a ring-necked pheasant has 18, and a grouse has 16. These feathers are also molted in pairs, so you may be hard pressed to find a bird with an odd number of tail feathers.

Before you carve a bird with spread tail feathers, you want to check the exact count necessary for the bird you are carving. These tail feathers are called rectrices. You will note that the quills are more to the center of the central tail feathers, and move more to the outside of the outer tail feathers where structurally they add greater strength to the tail for support and maneuverability during flight. These feathers not only provide lift in flight and behave as an air brake on landing, but also act together as a rudder to help steer the bird left or right. The primary wing feathers (ten on each wing) are stacked and structured in much the same way, and when viewed from this perspective, it becomes very clear how and why the feathers we consider so fragile can sustain migratory birds for thousands of miles of flight.

Figure 5 - Feathers Carved With Sharp Squared Edges

Figure 6 - Feathers Carved With Realistic Rolled Edges

Know Your Game Laws!

A word of caution about the possession of reference birds such as songbirds, birds of prey, shorebirds, and migratory birds, whether mounted, as study skins, or frozen. A state and federal permit is required. Fines can be very severe for offenders. Check with your state's Fish and Wildlife Department, as well as your nearest Federal Fish and Wildlife Office. Gain a complete and legal understanding of what is necessary to acquire permits to obtain and possess birds, bird skins, or even feathers, before you decide to build a collection of dead birds as references to support your art form.

Sources for Study Birds

Other sources to consider for study references are museums, colleges, universities, bird societies, and nature complexes that have study collections and educational permits and are willing to share. Many have lending programs where you can borrow the skin of a bird to study both for carving and painting. The university I use allows me to borrow three skins at a time. I check them out just like books from a library, and when I bring them back (in good condition!), I can borrow others. As a rule, the university prefers not to loan mounted birds because of the fragility and ease of damage during transportation.

Feather Shape

One thing woodcarvers often lose sight of is the cupped and bent shape of feathers (see **Figure 5** and **Figure 6**). The feather, as a rule, is a rounded mound on the exposed or upper side, and cupped on the hidden or lower side, especially the body or contour feathers. The working feathers such as the primaries, secondaries, tertials, scapulars, and tail feathers also have a cupped shaped when viewed from the end, although some may flare upward away from the cup on their edges where they rest against feathers beneath them. Woodcarvers seem to drift toward the sharp, square-edged position that house shingles represent instead of creating the mounded rolling look of real feathers.

Figure 7A - Typical Upper Wing Feather Groups

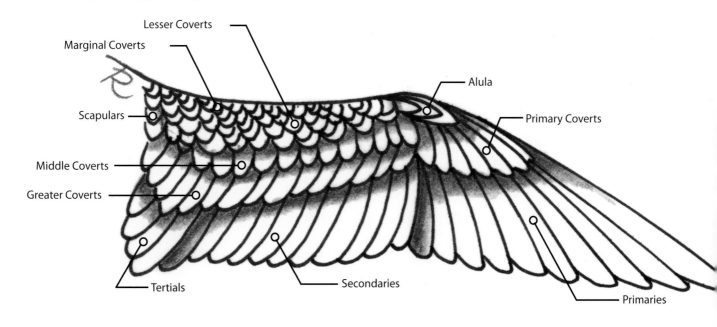

Lesser Coverts
Marginal Coverts
Scapulars
Middle Coverts
Greater Coverts
Tertials
Secondaries
Alula
Primary Coverts
Primaries

Figure 7B - Typical Underwing Feather Groups

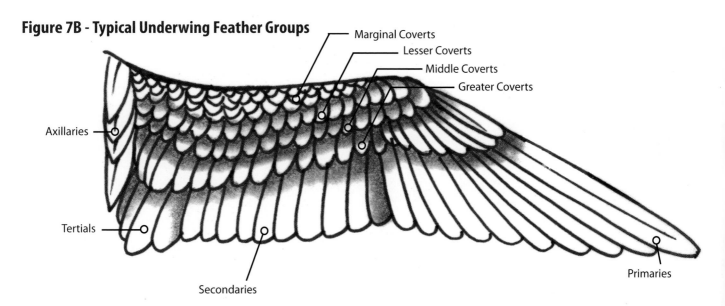

Marginal Coverts
Lesser Coverts
Middle Coverts
Greater Coverts
Axillaries
Tertials
Secondaries
Primaries

While you are viewing the harder, sharper flight feather groups, note the contours and shapes of the softer cover feather groups. Further note the contours formed within these groups by feathers that align in little groups of three or four, and others that separate themselves from the aligned ones. The "bumps" and "rolls" are endless. You will very quickly begin to formulate a method and technique as to how you want to lay out, carve, detail, and texture these same groups (and individual feathers) on your carving. When you get an idea as to how certain feathers lie, draw

them! I hear a lot of grumbling from some of my students during bird carving seminars when I have them take the time to draw on paper certain feather concepts that seem to be giving them problems during feather layout on a carving. After much shifting, erasing, and snorting, they finally draw feathers and feather placement to their (and my) satisfaction. As an instructor, I enjoy seeing the transition from frustration to relaxed enjoyment as they gradually grasp the concept of feather layout.

Feather Groups

Primaries are big, strong, heavy-shafted feathers that contribute the most to flight (see **Figure 7A** and **Figure 7B**). Usually ten in number per wing, they are most conspicuous when extended in flight; however, they are still very visible when the wing is folded. The exposed portion of the primary group very much affects the contour of the bird's back—more so on birds with longer pointed wings, such as hawks or swifts, than on birds with rounded wingtips, such as grouse or cardinals.

Secondaries are a continuation of the primary group, along the trailing edge of the wing. Like the wings of an airplane, they provide lift and stabilize the bird's flight.

Tertials are the group of innermost secondaries closest to the body. They are usually of different shape, longer, and often a different color.

Wing coverts are feathers on both the topside and underside of the wings. On the topside, the primary coverts overlap the primaries, and the greater coverts overlap the secondaries. The primary and greater coverts are in turn overlapped by the middle coverts, that in turn are overlapped by the lesser coverts which cover to and around the leading edge of the wing. On the underside are rows of longish feathers, called the wing lining, that overlap both primaries and secondaries. The wing lining is overlapped by lesser coverts that extend and blend into the wing's leading edge and into the lesser coverts from topside.

Alula (AL-you-la) corresponds to the thumb at the joint farthest out on the front of a bird's wing. It acts as a wind slot, like trim tabs and ailerons on an airplane. The feathers are called quills and may vary from two to seven or more on some species. (The average number for waterfowl and birds of prey is three.)

Axillars, also called axillaries, are the innermost feathers on the underside of the wing next to the body. They are usually elongated in shape and are located over what would be the armpit. They fill the space between the body and the wings when the wings are spread, and can't be seen when the wing is folded.

Scapulars are usually elongated feathers that arise from the bird's shoulders on either side of the back and adjacent to each wing where they overlap the tertials and wing coverts. They help cover the folded wings, and assist in streamlining the body/wing juncture during flight. They may be of a different color or demarcation, as are the surrounding feathers.

Forehead is the area immediately above the top of the bill and the crown (see **Figure 8** and **Figure 9**).

Crown is the area on top of the head between the forehead and the occiput.

Figure 8 - Typical Songbird Feather Groups

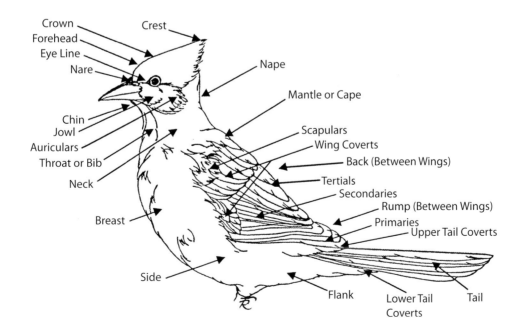

Occiput (OK-sih-put) is the back part of the head or skull.

Nape is the back part of the neck below the head.

Eye line or valley is a very pronounced indentation where the crown and forehead above meet the jowl and auriculars below to form a valley in which the eye is located. This is an important part of the head that deserves study. Not considering this area is why many beginning carvers create misplaced eyes and/or bug-eyed birds.

Jowl includes minuscule feathers that cover the area where the upper and lower mandibles (the beak) join. It sits just ahead of the auriculars and can often be evidenced by a slight depression before the auriculars begin. There is often a distinct demarcation on many waterfowl and larger bird species.

Auriculars are loosely webbed feathers on the sides of the head that cover the ear openings. If you look closely, you will find that this group (often called the ear coverts) is prominent.

Bib or Jugulum is the lower throat and that part just above the breast.

Mantle or Cape is the plumage on the back of the bird just below the nape. Ornithologically, the mantle also includes the top wing coverts.

Taxidermy Mount Problems

Be careful if you plan to use mounted birds as reference. The taxidermist can make errors, and you may incorporate his errors into your carving. One of the first ducks I ever purchased for a reference was a taxidermy mount of a standing canvasback drake with wings mounted outside of the sidepockets! My lack of knowledge at the time caused me to purchase an inaccurate mount and carve an inaccurate bird from it. I later found that the shape of the mounted head was wrong, too. I put trust in someone else's work because I had not taken the time to learn it myself. The main lesson I learned from that effort was not to do it again.

Chest/Breast/Belly includes usually rounded, soft contour feathers that begin below the bib and extend downward and around to meet the side and flank feathers. There are at least three important things to observe within these areas: the general shape of the feather, the look of softness, and the overall size of the feathers that get progressively larger as they progress through the chest into the breast and begin to diminish as they near the flank.

Side includes large, rounded, and fanned contour feathers. They are very conspicuous for size and softness and, depending on species, are strikingly marked on some species, especially waterfowl. This group is often called the side pocket on waterfowl because as the duck lands and folds its wing, the folded wing is set inside the flap formed by these feathers. Songbird wings do not enjoy the extent of coverage and support from the side feathers that waterfowl do, so study placement before you carve your bird's wings.

Figure 9 - Typical Waterfowl Feather Groups

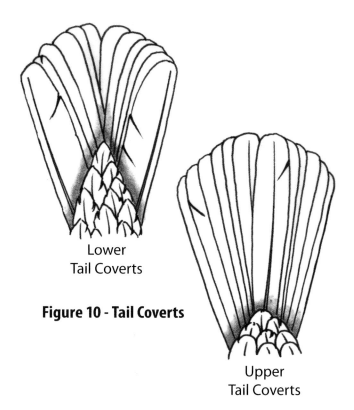

Figure 10 - Tail Coverts

Lower
Tail Coverts

Upper
Tail Coverts

Flank includes feathers that run back from the belly to become the undertail coverts, and up either side to meet the rump. If anything, these feathers are softer, yet often have a coarser appearance because of the rougher treatment they get from whatever the bird walks through, swims through, or perches on.

Rump includes the back feathers that lie below the wings and extend back to blend with the upper tail coverts.

Tail Coverts, upper and lower, cover and protect the bases of the tail feathers. Of importance to the carver is the extent to which they extend onto the upper part and lower side of the tail. Normally, the lower tail coverts extend onto the tail much farther and form a different shape than do the upper tail coverts (see **Figure 10**), a point beginning carvers often fail to notice. Also of importance is how the feathers are shaped, and how they overlap as they cover their portion of the tail.

Figure 11 - Typical Feather Flow Lines

Tail feathers are spread when maneuverability is needed during flight. They are not usually greatly spread when the bird is perched and at rest, unless it is preening, stretching, or displaying. However, a bit of artistic license can be taken to exemplify this feather group by spreading them enough to show the exposed area of the stems, barbs, and other feather detail such as splits and overlays.

Take the time to learn what happens to the tail when the bird is involved in the activity and pose that you wish to carve it in. The tail is extremely important to you as a carver because its position generally reflects the bird's activity. You must know what the tail does during these activities for the specific bird you are carving—activities such as normal flight, landing, at rest, displaying, preening, and defending. A good example of a special situation is mantling by birds of prey, such as a kestrel mantling over a mouse it had just caught. A bird of prey will mantle over its catch to keep it from being stolen by other predators. The body lowers into a crouch, then the wings and tail are spread down and over its catch.

Feather Layout

Before feathers can be drawn and finish carved, you must have some idea as to what you want the feathers to do and where you want them to go directionally. An understanding of how the feather tracts meet and meld to cover the bird's body is important before you can accurately draw and carve them.

Flow lines are lines drawn within the feather groups to assist the texturing process and maintain proper direction of feathers as they are laid out on a bird. It takes some study of the subject bird to establish proper direction so the feathers flow or bend not only within their group, but also overlap or join with neighboring groups to gracefully cover the whole bird.

On a duck, feather direction flows typically as shown on the sketch (see **Figure 11**).

Think of the bird as completely covered, but give each feather group proper direction within that covering.

In most cases, there are very distinct and noticeable division and contour lines between the major feather groups, but even though these lines exist, the feathers still maintain grace and direction. I mention grace because I believe it is important to note that some carvers are intent on showing the demarcation of the feather groups without giving enough care to how the meeting feathers interact and join to cover the bird.

Some beginning carvers are so concerned with establishing the various groups for the observer that they make the joining of the groups almost impossible with regard to how the feathers might lie on the actual bird.

Feather Placement and Size

Many beginning carvers are told that feathers shingle one over the other; this is true, but unfortunately they lay out their feathers exactly like shingles—straight, evenly spaced, and staggered, one over the other, row after row, course after course, with little if any variation (see **Figure 12**).

Although feathers lie one over another, the vast majority are not in rows and are different sizes. Feathers, like human hairs, are always in a state of replacement and growth because some are always being shed or pulled or preened. (Now that I'm slightly older, I notice this phenomenon more and more on my comb and in my hairbrush . . . although I wait in vain for the replacement parts.)

Because of this constant change, don't be afraid to draw small feathers with and atop the larger ones within a particular feather group. This applies most particularly to the softer, nonworking feathers such as head, neck, breast, cape, flank, belly, and lower tail coverts. Typically, a group of feathers would be sketched like **Figure 13**. This mixing of feather sizes doesn't necessarily apply to the working (flight) feathers, such as primaries, secondaries, and tail. Although the change occurs, it isn't as readily noticeable because of the way the feathers are laid or stacked one atop the other. Feather ends and varying sizes of feathers are not as obvious as the smaller, softer, more visually exposed feathers.

Feather Life

Feathers must be given life in order to be attractive and flow with the group. Feathers that look stiff and straight, even though they have direction (flow), detract from a carving. I sketch a central flow line in the middle of each feather not only to create direction for layout of the entire bird, but also to keep me on track for direction of strokes while I am texturing—whether with a texturing stone or a woodburner. How well I plan these little guidelines is directly proportional to what the finished feathers do, and ultimately the final and overall appearance of the carving. For comparison, I use the previous feather layout sketch and show it with no life (see **Figure 14**), and then add life by giving each feather within the group a directional flow of its own (see **Figure 15**).

How Many Feathers?

Though it is not necessary to know an exact feather count as a woodcarver, it is interesting to note the number on some birds. More or less, a mallard duck has 12,000 feathers, while a whistler swan has 25,000. A ruby-throated hummingbird has 940 feathers, but proportionately it has more feathers per body weight than the whistler swan. Songbirds will have from 1,200 to 4,600 feathers, while the stately bald eagle, for all of its size, has fewer than 7,200. The feathers on that same eagle will have a total weight of 1¼ pounds, which is more than double the weight of the bird's entire skeleton.

Practice

Take the time to observe feathers, and then practice drawing different feather shapes, individual feathers, and groups of feathers until you are satisfied that what you have drawn represents the feathers you want to carve and texture.

Figure 12 - Shingled Feather Layout

Figure 13 - Feather Layout Lines

Figure 14 - Feather Layout with No Life

Figure 15 - Feather Layout with Life and Direction

Creating Hard Feathers

By Frank Russell

Burning Tips:

• If you don't feel a degree of contact with the wood, chances are you are burning too hot and will have a charred surface.

• If you feel too much friction and drag with each stroke, you are burning too cool and are not getting sufficient depth to your stroke. You will soon get tired because of the amount of pressure needed to achieve texture.

• Begin at the bottom and work upward.

• Begin at the rear and work forward.

• To maintain continuity, occasionally allow your stroke to run in the same direction as the previously textured feather below it.

Always use a light to cast a shadow across the area opposite the texturing hand. For example: If you are right-handed, position the light on your left. Every time you stroke, the light will cast a shadow on the depression, which allows you to see the progress of the texturing.

The assortment of tools I use to create hard feathers are: (top to bottom) bent skew burning tip (dull), straight skew burning tip (sharp), ball-shaped stone, flame-shaped ruby carver, tapered steel bit, 1" (2.5cm)-diameter defuzzing pad (hard), 2" (5.1cm)-diameter rotary brush (soft), and tapered sanding mandrel with cloth-backed sandpaper.

Hard feathers are ones that help achieve flight and maneuvering. They include primaries, secondaries, and tail feathers. Other feathers are included that sometimes embrace tertials and scapulars, depending on the species of bird and whether I want the feather to look hard.

In order to achieve a hard-looking feather, I finish texture using a burning system. The burn lines give a stiffer, more rigid appearance caused by the shallow evenness and close repetition of the burning strokes. I like a marked, but not obtrusive, differentiation between the hard feather groups and the softer-appearing feather groups found on the breast, flank, and belly.

Feather Details

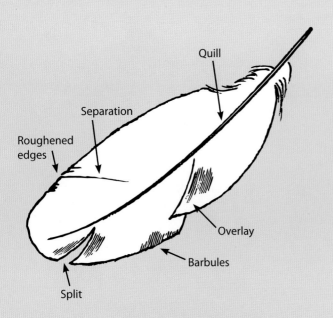

A **split** is a barbule separation that leaves a V-shaped opening in the feather, revealing a part of the feather below. A split is a great place to call attention to your work because not only is there a carved detail but also a place to accentuate when you paint. This is where you are able to create additional highlighting and shading on the feather.

A **separation** is a lesser split. A bird's natural movement causes a feather's barbules to separate. But the barbules realign without the hooklike barbecells interlocking as they do when the bird preens. The appearance is simply one of a deeper groove between the barbules. Try to establish these separations where feather groups work against or into one another.

An **overlay** is a separation that goes the opposite way of a conventional split. Instead of an open V shape, the upper barbules lay over the lower barbules. This creates a notch in the edge of the feather and a raised ledge where the overlay runs back to join the quill. An overlay is a nice place to draw attention to your skills. However, an overlay occurs much less frequently than a split, so don't overdo it.

Keep in mind that splits or separations can also be overdone. A few are natural, but as a rule many indicate either a sick or stressed bird. Even a storm-blown bird will preen and realign feathers before it sleeps rather than allow the feathers to go in disrepair.

1 *Define the feather groups.* I first make sure the outer edges of a feather group appear to roll over or under the adjacent groups as they do on the real bird. I finish sand the surface to a point that allows me to easily lay out the feathers. Essentially, I give particular attention to removing all tool marks, but I maintain the shape of the overall group with a smooth and finish-sanded appearance.

2 *Lay out the feather group pattern with a pencil.* Take time to draw exactly the shape and size of feathers you want to create. If the feathers don't appear the way I want them to, I erase and redraw them. This is the foundation not only for the finished appearance of the feather group, but also for the overall appearance of the bird carving. To stress the importance of the penciled layout stage, I tell my students that one of the most important tools a woodcarver has is a pencil, and the next most important tool is the rubber eradicator on the end of that pencil.

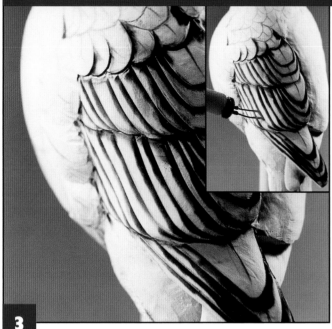

3 ***Outline the lower edges.*** With a bent skew burning tip (see inset), outline the lower edge of each feather within the group. I always test the intensity of the heat on a piece of scrap wood of the same species I am carving. This gives me an accurate and reliable indication of the heat setting I need.

4 ***Lay out the exposed quills or feather shafts and shaft tips.*** Draw the bent skew tip along each side of the quill. I practice this motion on the scrap wood until I can achieve the thickness and size of the quill desired at the body end and the point that ends before the outer tip of the feather. For comfort sake, I find that drawing the burner tip toward my body creates a better feel and sense of control. I also locate and relieve feather splits, separations, and overlays now (see Feather Details on page 52).

5 ***Finish shape and remove any sharp feather edges.*** I can achieve shaping by drawing away from the quill with the bent skew burner tip to contour the feather barbs. I break down and shape sharp edges by drawing the tip along the feather edges with a lower heat setting or I very lightly stroke the sharp edges with a defuzzing pad on a rotary mandrel.

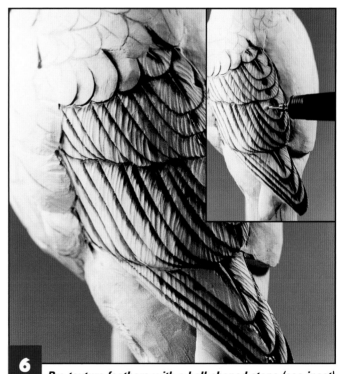

6 ***Pre-texture feathers with a ball-shaped stone (see inset).*** This gives shape and initiates motion in the feathers. By pre-texturing, I establish direction, feather shape, and the amount of curve the barbules will have on each feather when I burn. Don't overdo this step. Also, the pre-texture strokes don't have to be loose or numerous.

7 ***Texture feathers with a straight skew burner tip.*** Again, I practice on scrap wood, setting the heat at the optimum temperature for the cadence of strokes suitable to my method of burning (see Burning Tips on page 51).

8 ***Remove high spots and sharp edges.*** If I observe any high spots or sharp edges that were missed in the previous step, or were created as a result of the burning, I reduce them by gently stroking with a defuzzing pad. If I apply too much pressure, I risk obliterating the texturing entirely.

FEATHERS: CLEANING THE CARVING

9 ***Clean the textured area with a soft rotary brush.*** My strokes are in the direction of the texturing to lessen any loss of texture. I use either a 1" or 2" (2.5cm or 5.1cm)-diameter soft bristle brush at a low speed to achieve a nice scrubbing action. This operation is necessary before sealing and gessoing the project prior to applying the color. If any dust or wood char is left on the textured area, a small bump is created. If not removed, it will be sealed and increased in size by the gesso and the painting process. I take my carving out in harsh sunlight and turn it, looking for dirt, lumps, bumps, or any other details I may have missed.

10 ***Seal the carving.*** Prior to gessoing, I seal my carvings with clear matte finish automotive lacquer thinned 50% with lacquer thinner. If I run out of or can't find automotive lacquer, I use matte finish Deft, thinned with the same proportion of lacquer thinner. I use a large, soft bristle brush and let the carving absorb as much as it wants up to a usual two or three coats. I dry the surface thoroughly between coats with a hair dryer.

Texturing Strategies for Bird Carvers

By Lori Corbett

Obviously, good anatomy and having the right colors are essential to carving realistic birds, but lurking beneath the pose and paint is another key ingredient: texture.

In the early days of bird carving, carvers painted the look of texture on each bird. Then, carvers used soldering irons to capture feather anatomy. Today, micro grinders and woodburners are in every bird carver's tool kit. Once you see what grinding and burning can accomplish, you won't want to use anything else.

In the Heat of Realism

The soul of a burning unit may be the rheostat box that controls the temperature, but the heart is the tip. Pictured at right are seven burning pen tips:

1. **Angled blade with a rounded heel.** My favorite tip, it is excellent for making short, fine lines on areas such as head feathers.

2. **Extended curved blade.** It's a great choice for tight, round areas represented in the cape-to-neck transition on waterfowl.

3. **Spear pen.** My preferred tip for helping to undercut primary feathers.

4. **Scribe point.** I use this one to sign my name.

5. **Angled blade ³⁄₁₆" (5mm) wide.** It can't be beat for long, sweeping feathers, and it is my second favorite tip.

6. **Bent angled blade.**

7. **Bent angled blade with rounded heel.** Both this and the previous tip I bent myself to reach under raised feathers, such as primaries. The bend allows me to keep the knife-like edge of the tip at a 90° angle to my burning surface. Because I am right-handed, the tips are bent to the right (see photo at right). Southpaws need to bend the tips in the opposite direction.

An array of burning pen tips that contribute to textured surfaces on wildfowl.

Scratch It? Sand It!

Thorough sanding is the most important preparation you can accomplish prior to grinding and burning. Any scratches left on the wood will show through the subsequent texturing and painting. My sanding strategy is as follows: The first step is an overall sanding with a small rotary drum attachment in either a flexible shaft machine or a micro grinder. I then use cloth-backed sandpaper—Swiss Red is ideal—starting with 80 or 100 grit and working through 120-, 150-, 220-, 320-, and finally 500-grit paper. I make sure to sand in the direction of the grain as much as possible.

When using grits that are 220 or finer, I don't apply too much pressure because even fine paper can leave scratches. To get rid of unwanted marks, I start the sanding process over, beginning with a coarse grit such as 120.

Making Stiff, Soft, and Intermediate Feathers

Figure 1 illustrates the parts of a feather with which you should be familiar. The backbone of a feather is its shaft. Individual structures called barbs emerge from both sides of the shaft. Collectively the barbs are called vanes.

There are generally three types of feathers found on all birds, in addition to specialty feathers.

1. **Major flight feathers**–their edges are very definite and have a smooth, hard look to them.

2. **Soft feathers**–usually found on the belly, flanks, sides, head, and sometimes the breast. They are often bunched, and their shapes will vary greatly.

3. **Intermediate feathers**–fall somewhere in between the hard and soft feathers and typically make up the scapulars, back, cape coverts—both wing and tail—and sometimes the breast. They have a definite edge as the stiff feathers have, but the edges are somewhat closer, although not nearly as close as the soft feathers (see **Figure 2**).

Two steps follow on the next page for making stiff, soft, and intermediate feathers.

Sanding supplies for smoothing surfaces in your birds include cloth-backed paper, sanding sticks, a sanding drum, and Scotch-Brite.

Figure 2

Stiff Feather
Sharp delineated edges. Holds its shape well.

Soft Feather
Soft and whispy edges, sometimes furlike, such as on the breast and belly of raptors.

Intermediate Feather
Holds its shape but edges are softer than the stiff feathers.

Figure 1: Anatomy of a Feather

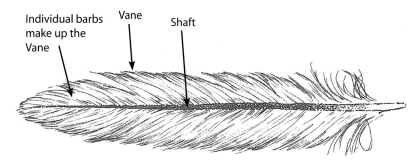

Individual barbs make up the Vane

Vane

Shaft

1 **Layout the basic outlines.** The photo shows, clockwise from the upper right, a stiff, an intermediate, and a soft feather. Notice the slight S curves of the pencil lines. The curves become longer and more sweeping as the feathers get increasingly softer.

2 **Texture then burn.** Except for the stiff feather, texture each feather prior to burning. For super-fine, tight burning on all feathers, burn at a low temperature, doing little more than scoring the wood. Burned wood should be a golden brown color. For the soft feather, the texturing and burning extend unevenly past the initial outline. On an actual carving, this texture extends into the underlying feathers. For the intermediate feather, the texturing and burning do not extend as far past the outline, giving the feather an even edge, a trait of stiff feathers.

Laying Out Feather Groups

Unless you intend to carve an individual feather for display or ornamentation, you need to look at a bird in terms of feather groups. How you lay out these groups is just as important as how you texture them. A common mistake is to draw them all the same size as well as evenly spaced. I call this problem "soldiering." The feathers line up in neat rows like soldiers at attention. In **Figure 3**, you can see two groups of breast feathers. The group on the left is soldiered. The group on the right has a more pleasing flow because the feathers vary in size and direction. Yet, they still follow the flow pattern of the overall breast feather group.

Feather flow is also affected by the fact that birds are continually losing feathers and new ones are growing in to replace them. If feathers are out of place or there are small variations of shape, they appear to flow in a different direction from their neighbors. Softer feather groups tend to flow in bunches. How much depends on the species and feather group. On a waterfowl, the breast feathers bunch up less than the looser side pocket feathers, for example. On some birds of prey, the breast and belly feathers are long and soft, so the bunching is more apparent. By laying out feather groups with this kind of variation, you are adding more interest and realism to your carving. Even groups that do tend to fall into orderly rows, such as the scapular and cape feathers, will benefit from a little variation in feather size and flow.

I recommend eight steps for texturing a breast area with both short and long feathers. The instructions here include feather flow, sanding, power carving individual feathers, and burning.

Figure 3

Flow Lines
Even though the feathers follow the flow lines, they're too orderly and boring.

Flow Lines
These feathers are less orderly, sized differently, and oriented in different directions, yet still follow the flow lines.

Figure 4

Straight texturing lines. Wrong.

C curve texturing lines. Note how the direction of the barbs vary slightly from one feather to the next.

Texturing the Breast Area

1 ***Begin by establishing the flow of the breast area.*** It is the direction in which the feathers grow as a group. Draw the flow lines with a graphite pencil.

2 ***Lay out feather bunches following the general direction of the flow lines.*** For the short, soft feathers on the left, these bunches resemble teardrops. On long, soft feathers, the bunches resemble flames.

3 ***Carve grooves.*** Use a flame-shaped ruby carver or diamond bit to carve along these lines to form a groove. Make them shallower on the short, soft feather bunches and deeper on the longer, looser feather bunches. The process is called landscaping because hills and valleys, also called lumps and bumps, are created. Blend the bunches by using the same carving bit to knock off the hard edges of the grooves and create gentle depressions from one bunch to another. Do not leave hard edges that look like steps. After sanding them smooth, redraw the flow lines.

4 ***Fill in the feathers.*** Treating each bunch separately, draw the individual feathers, following the flow lines. In the case of the long, fur-like feathers on the right, draw smaller flame shapes. Make the feathers different sizes, but do not vary them too greatly. Occasionally draw one out of place, flowing in a direction slightly different from its neighbors. When done, step back and look at the overall layout. Adjust anything that appears to "soldier." Note that each bunch has its own varying flow pattern that is slightly different from the others, yet it still follows the overall flow of the major grouping.

5 ***Grind the feathers.*** For the group on the left, use a blunt tapered diamond bit on its side to grind in the individual feathers. Work from the bottom bunch to the top bunch. Within each bunch, work from bottom feather to top feather. For the group on the right, use a flame-shaped ruby carver or a diamond bit. Then, use a ball-nose diamond bit to knock down the hard edges, making smooth, soft bumps. Notice the V-shaped areas at the intersection of some feather groups. Each is a great place to add interest. Using a small, long-tapered diamond bit, relieve the area in the point of the V and blend it out to the feather edge. Incise the V and run it under the edges of the adjacent and overlapping feathers to "raise" them slightly. Sand first with a soft-backed sanding drum using light pressure; then, hand sand with the various grits mentioned earlier for texture preparation. On the short, soft feather bunches, you want to almost sand away the individual feathers, but not quite to the point where they disappear.

6 ***Redraw the individual feathers.*** For the second-to-last step prior to burning, redraw the individual feathers in the short, soft feather groups. Using a blue cone-shaped stone, grind in the feather barbs, varying their direction slightly. Use quick strokes to help maintain a light touch. Instead of making the barbs straight, grind them with small C-shaped curves (see **Figure 4** on page 57). Using a Scotch-Brite pad, lightly go over the texturing. Follow the direction of the barbs to knock off the sharp edges caused by the stone.

7 ***Finish the long soft feathers.*** Using a blue stone, grind in the feather barbs. Work from the outside of the feather in toward its center, following the contours (see **Figure 5**). Grind quickly, being careful not to apply too much pressure. Use the Scotch-Brite pad as you did in the previous step.

Making the Difference

Study your reference material—study skins, photos, live birds—as closely as you can to determine the kinds of feathers you are looking at. When you have a feel for the types, experiment with bunching feathers. When you have the techniques mastered, your carvings will progress to a new level of realism.

8 ***Burn in the texture, following the direction of the ground-in barbs.*** Use a low-temperature setting to prevent a deep burn. The result should be no darker than a golden brown. For short feathers, use an angled blade with a rounded heel. For longer, looser feathers use an angled blade ³⁄₁₆" (5mm) wide. Areas are left unburned for comparison. In some cases, it may be preferable not to burn at all—for example, the breast and belly of some birds of prey. Instead, seal the wood, and then paint after texturing. Leaving the area unburned creates a looser, softer texture.

The techniques used for the short, soft feathers can be applied to the larger soft feathers such as on the side pockets of waterfowl. The major difference is that instead of teardrop-shaped bunches, you draw long sweeping S curves and lay out the feathers between them (see **Figure 6**).

Figure 5

Texturing follows the shape of the "flame."

Figure 6

Flow lines as S curves.

Projects

The projects featured in this section are meant to allow you to practice the techniques shown earlier in the book and to provide you with an array of projects that can be done by carving with power. Hopefully, they will get you started in power carving generally, encourage you to try a different category of carving if you're already carving with power, or inspire you to design your own creations. Projects are ordered by difficulty.

Turning Over a New Leaf Carved Bowl, by Keoma McCaffrey, page 62.

Turning Over a New Leaf Carved Bowl

Upcycle a vintage wooden bowl with power-carved leaves

By Keoma McCaffrey

My passion as a woodcarver leaves me looking at every wooden surface as a blank canvas—backs of chairs, window frames, doors.... When my husband brought a wooden salad bowl home from a thrift store, he couldn't believe it when I said I was going to carve it. Then, when I finished it, served dinner in it, and told him I had already sold it, he loved it. The next thing I knew, he was bringing home boxes of bowls from wherever he could find them!

The bowl shown here was one of our pricier purchases—it cost $2. I have paid up to $3.99 for bowls, but my favorites cost $0.50 or $0.75. When I sell them at craft fairs, my prices start at $30, so I am very happy with that return on my investment!

Often made from teak, maple, or walnut, these bowls were popular in the 1960s and 1970s, and are easy to find at thrift stores and yard sales. It was popular at the time for bowls to have thick sides, which makes them easy to carve. While I demonstrate on a bowl that has ½" (13mm)-thick sides, you can use a bowl with thinner sides, or even create a pierced relief design.

Safety

When carving these vintage bowls, wear a dust mask. Some finishes from the 1970s and before contained lead, which will be released when we carve though the finish; a mask will keep you from breathing any dangerous particles. Also, because we're power carving, wear goggles and protect your fingers with Finger Pro Safety Tape, available from Woodcarvers Supply (*www.woodcarversupply.com*, 800-284-6229). The tape sticks only to itself, but it stops burs and bits from chewing up my hands.

Getting Started

The first step is to transfer the patterns to the bowl. I literally pick leaves off trees and trace around them, but we've included patterns, as well. Size the patterns appropriately for your bowl, and trace around them with a permanent marker. I also traced a skinny branch onto the leaves and sketched a few acorns to fill big open spaces.

BOWL: ROUGHING OUT THE LEAVES

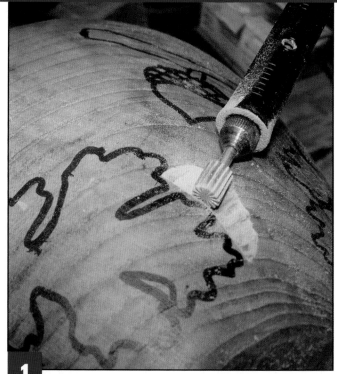

1 *Outline the leaves.* Chuck a cylinder-shaped fluted bit in a rotary tool, pick a spot, and start outlining the leaves. This can be time consuming, but it helps define and protect the leaves.

2 *Remove the background material.* Use a large, fine-grit, ball-shaped carbide-point bit. Remove all of the excess wood between the leaves and around the branch and acorn.

3 ***Refine the edges of the leaves.*** Use the tip of a bull-nose, tapered, fluted bit to carve a shallow trench around the edges of each element to separate them from the background. Use the side of the same bit to blend the outer edges of the trenches with the background. Sand off any remaining marker lines.

4 ***Shape the leaves.*** Use the large, fine-grit, ball-shaped, carbide-point bit. Start at the tip of each leaf node. Move from the node to the stem in a smooth downward motion to give each leaf movement and texture.

This technique works on any size bowl or wooden accessory; just vary the sizes of the leaves. You can also place and carve leaves along the top of a bowl to form a patterned edge. Have fun experimenting!

SANDPAPER JIG

I used to buy precut sandpaper circles, but I went through them so fast I started making my own. Start with a roughly torn circle of sandpaper (I am using 80-grit). Punch a hole in it with a mandrel head screw. Use a few old circles of sandpaper as washers. Position a small washer on the top, and then the rough circle of sandpaper, and a few washers on the bottom. Start the rotary tool with the mandrel pointing away from your face, and then press it lightly to your work surface or a scrap piece of hardwood. It spins so fast that the sandpaper turns into a perfect circle and at the same time leaves a beautiful burnt groove.

5 *Add the leaf veins.* Place the sandpaper jig at the base of a leaf, close to the stem, and slowly move it toward the tip of the leaf. Then, working in the groove you just made, place the paper at the fork to a new leaf node and slowly work toward the end again. If that one splits off, do the same, following it to the end. The veins get smaller as you go, so carve the bigger lines first because the sandpaper shrinks as you use it.

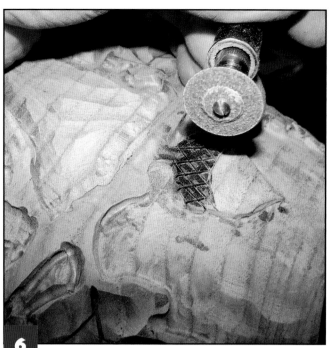

6 *Carve and detail the acorn.* Use the technique explained in Step 4 to shape the bottom of the acorn, carving off the outline. Then use the process from Step 5 to carve a diamond pattern on the acorn cap. After carving the lines, hold the sanding jig at a slight angle and remove the sharp corners from the individual diamonds to give them a 3D look.

7 *Smooth the background.* I use a large, fluted carbide cutter to remove the marks from the fine carbide-point bit. Sand the entire bowl with a fine-grit sanding sponge.

8 *Apply the finish.* I mix lavender essential oil with olive oil. The lavender keeps the olive oil from turning rancid, and it smells nice. Over time, the oil will antique itself, but you can bring the finish back to life with another application of oil. On occasion, if the detail is very deep or very detailed, I will use a salad bowl finish or a spray gloss finish, such as Krylon, on the outside to make it easier to keep the dust out of the nooks and crannies.

Bowl leaf patterns

© 2014 Woodcarving Illustrated

Making a Comfort Bird

Smooth lines and a polished finish make these little birds a joy to hold

By Frank Foust

Sized to fit in your palm and sanded silky smooth, these birds make a perfect gift or fund-raising project. Create the birds from any hardwood—I choose mine for the beauty of the grain. I hope you'll make several birds and share them with anyone who needs a bit of comfort.

1 *Cut away the excess wood.* Create templates by transferring the patterns to thin cardboard and cutting around the outline of the patterns. Trace the templates onto the blank and cut the top view of the bird with a band saw. Tape the waste in place, rotate the blank 90°, and cut the side view.

BIRD: CARVING THE PROJECT

2 *Rough out the bird.* Remove the sharp edges and rough shape the bird with a sanding drum equipped with 60-grit sandpaper. I use a 1½" (38mm)-diameter drum attached to a radial arm saw, but you can use a rotary-power carver. Shape the neck with a 1" (25mm)-diameter cushioned sanding drum.

3 *Finish shaping the bird.* Use a carving knife to shape the beak. Use a rotary-power carver and your bit of choice to add any desired details and to remove any remaining ridges. Make sure the bird is smooth and flowing with no hard lines or sharp angles.

BIRD: FINISHING THE PROJECT

4 ***Sand the bird.*** Sand the bird by hand with 150-grit sandpaper. Then, buff the bird with synthetic steel wool until the carving is perfectly smooth. Don't rush the process. Creating a smooth surface is a vital step.

5 ***Apply polyurethane.*** Insert a darning needle into the bottom of the bird to give you something to hold. Then, apply a light coat of polyurethane to the carving and allow the finish to dry thoroughly. Buff the carving with synthetic steel wool, apply another coat of finish, and let the finish dry thoroughly.

6 ***Finish the bird.*** Rub the second coat of polyurethane with powdered pumice mixed with oil. Remove the oil and pumice, and then apply paste wax. Use a soft cloth to buff the wax to a high gloss.

Comfort bird patterns

© 2011 Woodcarving Illustrated

Materials & Tools

Materials:
- Hardwood, 2" (5.1cm) square: 4¼" (10.8cm) long
- Tape
- Sandpaper: 150-grit
- Scouring pad, such as Scotch-Brite
- Polyurethane: clear
- Pumice stone: 4F
- All-purpose household oil
- Paste wax

The author used these products for the project. Substitute your choice of brands, tools, and materials as desired.

Tools:
- Radial arm saw (optional)
- Band saw
- Knife
- Drum sander: 1½" (38mm)-diameter 60-grit
- Cushioned sanding drum: 1" (25mm)-diameter
- Rotary-power carver with small diamond bit
- Darning needle
- Small paintbrush
- Soft cloths

Wood Wizard Cypress Knee

By Frank Russell

Drawing the Pattern

No two cypress knees are the same size and shape; that's what makes carving found wood so much fun. But, this means that you can't just trace a pattern onto the blank. Instead, you need to draw the pattern on the blank. Lightly draw an egg shape the size of the face you feel fits on the particular surface you are about to carve. This is only a guide and will not be cut around. Draw a horizontal centerline across the center of the egg for the eye line. Divide this line into five equal parts, and draw the eye shapes (twice as wide as high) in the second and fourth spaces. Draw a vertical centerline through the egg shape from top to bottom.

Draw flowing S lines running to either side of the egg from the top central portion of the egg. The portion above the eye line and brows will be the forehead, and these S lines represent hair that will be flowing from a separation or part beginning at the top of the head and curling outward on the forehead to the temple zone. This hair will lie atop the beard and provides excellent opportunity to carve curls, overlays, and divisions of hair during a later operation. Measure the distance between the outer corners of the eyes. Measure this distance down from the eye line and mark the center of the bottom lip. The bottom of the nose is one eye length above this point.

Materials & Tools

Materials:
- Cypress knee of choice
- Clear satin finish lacquer
- Paste wax and soft cloth

Tools:
- Flame-shaped bit
- Flame-shaped ruby carver
- Cylindrical bit
- Inverted cone bit
- Flame-shaped diamond bit
- Small ball-shaped bit
- Rotary bristle brush or old toothbrush

1 *Carve along the eye line.* Use the tip of a flame-shaped carbide bit. Carve deep enough that you can shape the slope of the nose outward at the tip. Draw the arched line for the bottom of the brows, and continue the lines along the outer edges of the nose, sweeping them out into the mustache.

2 *Carve the slope of the nose down to the tip.* Use the side of the flame-shaped carbide bit. Use the point of the same bit to carve matching grooves along the brow line, alongside the nose, and along the mustache. The groove should be deeper along the sides of the nose and at the outer corners of the eyes.

3 *Draw the outer edges of the eye mounds.* These lines should include the entire lower lid area. Carve in the eye mounds. Use a draw stroke with the flame-shaped carbide bit. Carve along both lines to a depth that will satisfy the shallowest contours along the line (the most forward portion of the eye mound).

4 *Continue to rough shape eye mounds.* Maintain a symmetrical shape for both. Deepen the inner corners of the eye mounds where they blend into the bridge of the nose, and allow the outer end of each mound to blend into the temple area.

5 *Draw the shallow V shape of the tip of the nose.* Beware making this V too sharp; it governs the overall shape of the nose. I suggest a slope of about 15°. It is advisable to make the V shallow to begin with—it can always be sharpened.

6 *Cut the nose V.* Use an inverted cone or a flame-shaped ruby bit held at a high angle. Use care not to cut too deeply, as the mustache will be running up underneath the nose, and stock should be left for it.

7 ***Draw the nose shape.*** Draw a line perpendicular to the center-line across the nose one-third of the way up from the tip to locate the wings of the nose. Make sure the outer extremes are equal as you draw the wings of the nose. Then, draw the extremes of the bridge of the nose from the brow line down and around the ball of the nose.

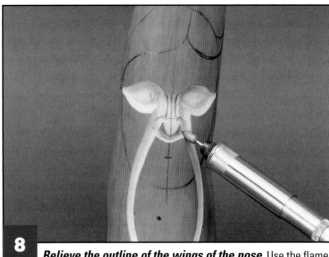

8 ***Relieve the outline of the wings of the nose.*** Use the flame-shaped ruby bit held at a high angle. Begin at the bottom, along the wing line, and finish with an angle at the bridge line.

9 ***Rough shape the nose.*** Use the flame-shaped ruby bit. Round the wings of the nose and blend gently into the ball of the nose. Use care, but remove any sharp edges. There are no sharp corners on the nose.

WIZARD: CARVING THE MOUTH AND BEARD

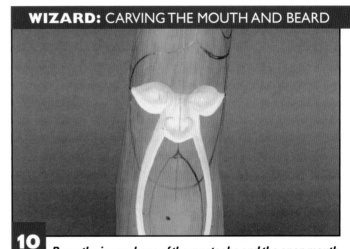

10 ***Draw the inner shape of the mustache and the open mouth.*** Carve along the lines with the flame-shaped carbide bit. Leave a little extra stock where the two inner sides of the mustache come together over the mouth. This extra stock will later become the lower lip.

11 ***Rough shape the mustache.*** Use the flame-shaped carbide bit.

12 ***Draw lines to represent the extremes of the beard on the cheeks.*** They run from the temple area down to the mustache just slightly below the nose. Draw the sides of the beard on the sides of the blank. They are below where the ears would be.

13 ***Cut in the extremes of the beard on the cheeks.*** Use the flame-shaped carbide bit. Be sure to use care in this area.

14 ***Cut in the lower extremes of the beard.*** Use random flowing drag strokes with the flame-shaped carbide bit. These go from the area below the curls of the forehead hair down to the beard tip.

WIZARD: CARVING THE CHEEKS AND EYES

15 ***Shape the cheeks and areas below the eyes.*** Use the flame-shaped ruby bit.

16 ***Shape the forehead from the hairline to the eyebrows and into the temples.*** Undercut the hair as necessary to raise it away from the skin. Leave a bit of extra stock in the area of the eyebrows to relieve away the size and shape of eyebrows that you want. Draw the eyebrow masses.

17 ***Relieve eyebrow masses.*** Use the flame-shaped ruby bit. Flow the edges into the forehead and lower brow arches. Rough shape beard and hair.

18 ***Reestablish the eye centerline and draw the finished shape of the eyes.*** Make sure both eyes are the same size and precisely located. Then, carve the eyes. Turn the corners up slightly to make the eyes look happy.

19 ***Draw matching nasolabial folds (smile lines).*** They start at the tops of the nose wings and head toward the corners of the mouth, ending at the top of the beard. Carve them with the flame-shaped ruby bit held at a 45˚ angle. Round and blend sides of folds. Finish shaping the cheeks, tear ducts, and temples with the same bit.

21 ***Draw the wrinkles.*** I add them to the corners of the eyes, forehead, brow, and below the eyes. Then, carve the wrinkles with the flame-shaped ruby bit. Smooth the edges so they don't appear exaggerated.

23 ***Texture all areas of hair.*** Start at the bottom of each area and working upward. No matter what scale of hair you decide on, either an inverted cone-shaped or cylinder-shaped bit is ideal for texturing. I find either bit gives essentially the same result. For coarser hair, use an aggressive (coarse) larger bit, and for finer hair, use a smaller, finer grit bit.

20 ***Draw the mouth.*** Use the flame-shaped ruby bit to carve the mouth opening and lower lip. Then, draw the nostril holes and carve the main hole with a ball-shaped bit. Use a small flame-shaped bit to carve the tail that curls up under the nose wing.

22 ***Evaluate the hair flow.*** Decide if you want any additional curls, separations, overlays, or raised areas. Then, carve these areas with your bit of choice before you add the hair texture. Then, draw the hair flow lines.

Finishing the Carving

Clean all areas with a rotary brush or a defuzzing pad. Use care—work in the direction of the texture and use a low rpm or you risk losing the texture detail. If you don't have a rotary brush, an old toothbrush can be used, though it takes a bit more effort to remove debris and fuzz. Seal the carving. Flow a coat of thinned, clear lacquer (satin finish) over the entire piece. Coat carving with a medium-light layer of paste wax. Buff just the high points by covering your hand with an old athletic sock and buffing with your hand held stiff.

Power Carving a Polar Bear

Develop your skills with this easy stylized design

By Chuck Solomon and Dave Hamilton

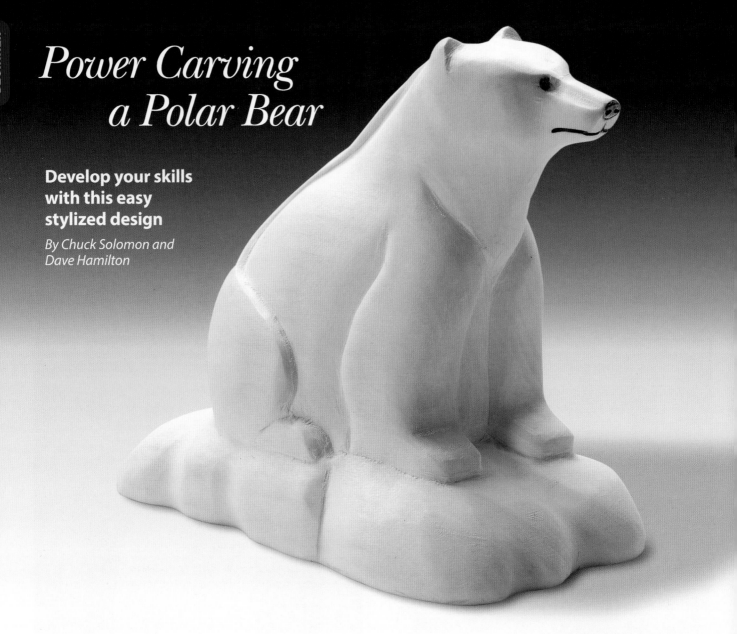

Stylized carvings make great beginner projects because you can focus on general form and technique without worrying about texturing or details. For those same reasons, stylized carving is a great change of pace for realistic carvers.

Most woodcarving shows have a category for stylized carving. It may be called stylized, interpretative, or abstract. Stylized carvings focus on the essence of the subject. For example, in this polar bear project, the overall body shape and profile of the head, as well as the snow base, define the subject as a polar bear.

Stylized carvings range from very simple to highly complex, sometimes incorporating paint and metals such as bronze or copper.

This pattern can be used to create a realistic polar bear carving by adding fur texture. Add texture with a white stone in a rotary-power carver or with veiners, V-tools, and other hand tools.

1 ***Transfer the pattern to the blank.*** Orient the wood grain parallel with the length of the head. Use graphite paper to transfer the profile to the blank or attach the pattern to card stock, cut around the pattern, and trace around the cut out. Cut the bear's profile with a band saw or coping saw.

POLAR BEAR: ROUGHING OUT

2 ***Draw the major landmarks.*** Draw a centerline on the body and mark the width of the major parts. Use the pattern as a guide. The head is turned to the left, so draw the centerline from the top of the head to the end of the muzzle. Sketch in the shape of the head.

3 ***Rough out the head.*** Use a 1" (25mm)-diameter extra coarse-grit carbide-point sleeve. Make several passes to remove the wood. Remove wood at the end of the muzzle to keep the head straight. Remove the waste around the muzzle and then around the head. The sides remain perpendicular to the top.

4 ***Rough out the body.*** Use a 1" (25mm)-diameter extra coarse-grit carbide-point sleeve. Remove wood at the neck, shoulders, rump, and base. Keep the lines straight at this point.

5 ***Round the body.*** Use a ¾" (19mm)-diameter coarse-grit carbide-point sleeve. Round the body starting at the neck. Work your way down the back to the rump and down the front to the base. Leave wood for the front feet.

POLAR BEAR: ADDING DEFINITION

6 ***Define the major elements.*** Draw in the front and back legs. Draw the S-shaped flow lines from the back legs to the back of the head. Keep the lines on the chest smooth and flowing. Carve along the lines with a ¼" (6mm)-diameter coarse-grit safe-end cylinder-shaped carbide-point bit.

7 ***Separate the front legs.*** Use a ⁹⁄₁₆" (14mm)-diameter fine-grit safe-end cylinder-shaped carbide-point bit to remove the wood between the front legs. Refine the area using a ¼" (6mm)-diameter fine-grit safe-end carbide-point bit.

8 *Carve the base.* Shape the snow under the bear with a ⁹⁄₁₆"-diameter (14mm) fine-grit safe-end cylinder-shaped carbide-point bit. Separate the snow into general masses, but keep the overall base smooth and rounded.

9 *Shape the head and define the ears.* Use a ¾" (19mm)-diameter coarse-grit carbide-point sleeve to lower the head in front of the ears. Make the cut perpendicular to the centerline on the head. Remove wood from between the ears with the same bit or a smaller carbide-point bit.

10 *Round the head and the muzzle.* Use a ¾" (19mm)-diameter coarse-grit carbide-point sleeve to round the head and the muzzle. Redraw the centerline as needed and keep the head symmetrical. Round the back of the ears.

POLAR BEAR: CARVING DETAILS

11 *Create the trough on the muzzle.* Use a ¼" (6mm)-diameter fine-grit safe-end cylinder-shaped carbide-point bit to create a trough on both sides of the muzzle. The eyes are located where the trough meets the head.

12 *Smooth and shape the head.* Use a bull nose-shaped ruby or diamond bit to remove wood in the center of the head and above the eyes. Create a shallow depression across the top of the head.

13 ***Draw in the facial details.*** Use the pattern and your own reference photos as a guide. Draw in the nose, mouth, and eyes with a soft lead pencil.

14 ***Refine the carving.*** Use a ¼" (6mm)-diameter fine-grit safe-end cylinder-shaped carbide-point bit to refine the flow lines and further define the ears, front legs, paws, and the snow drifts.

POLAR BEAR: SANDING AND BURNING

15 ***Sand the bear.*** Use 150- to 220-grit cloth-backed sandpaper in a cushioned sanding drum. Remove the tool marks from the carbide-point bits and refine the shape of the bear.

16 ***Woodburn the nose, mouth, and eyes.*** Use skew-tip and writing-tip burning pens to burn the nose, mouth, and eyes. Shade the nose and eyes with a curved-tip burning pen.

17 ***Deepen the nostrils.*** Use an awl or a tool with a sharp point to make a pilot hole for the nostrils. Plunge a pointed diamond or ruby bit into the wood to make a shallow nostril. The nostril should be a little more than ¹⁄₁₆" (2mm) deep.

18 ***Hand sand the bear.*** Use 220- to 250-grit cloth-backed sandpaper. Clean up any areas that need further refinement. Remove any cross-grain scratches. Remove the dust with a tack cloth or compressed air.

BEGINNER

Finishing the Carving

You can finish the carving with a few coats of Deft satin spray finish, but we chose to lighten the wood using a wood bleach. Wear safety glasses and rubber gloves and apply the bleach according to the manufacturer's instructions. Apply one to three coats of the bleaching solution—one coat every 10 minutes—and allow the bleach to remain on the carving for 1½ hours. Neutralize the bleach by brushing a coat of baking soda mixed with water over the entire carving. Allow the carving to dry for 24 hours. Apply a coat of Deft satin spray finish to the carving. Allow the Deft to dry for 45 minutes and rub the carving down lightly with 000 steel wool. Apply another coat of Deft, allow it to dry, and rub it down with steel wool. Apply a final coat of Deft, allow it to dry, and rub it lightly with steel wool.

Materials & Tools

Materials:
- Basswood, 4" (10.2cm) thick: 5½" x 6½" (14cm x 16.5cm)
- Cloth-backed sandpaper: 150 to 250 grits
- Graphite paper or card stock
- Wood bleach (optional)
- Finish: satin spray, such as Deft

Tools:
- Flexible-shaft machine
- Micromotor machine (optional)
- Coarse-grit carbide sleeve: ¾" (19mm) diameter
- Extra coarse-grit carbide-point sleeve: 1" (25mm) diameter
- Fine-grit safe-end cylinder-shaped carbide-point bit: 9/16" (14mm) diameter
- Coarse-grit safe-end cylinder-shaped carbide-point bit: ¼" (6mm) diameter
- Fine-grit safe-end cylinder-shaped carbide-point bit: ¼" (6mm) diameter
- Bull nose-shaped diamond or ruby bit
- Cushioned sanding drum
- Pointed diamond or ruby bit
- Band saw or coping saw
- Woodburner
- Burning pens: writing tip, ⅜" (10mm)-wide skew tip, ⅜" (10mm)-wide shader tip
- Paintbrush, flat: ½" (13mm) wide (to apply bleach)

Reference Material

The polar bear is tied with the Kodiak bear as the largest land carnivore. Polar bears are native to the Arctic Circle and live and hunt in the sea and on land. Polar Bears—Living with the White Bear *and* The World of the Polar Bear *are excellent reference books. Both titles include extensive biological and behavioral information and many high quality photographs. Internet searches are also a good source for reference photos.*

Polar bear patterns

Power Carving an American Bison in Relief

Learn the techniques to carve a gunstock on a less expensive wooden plate

By Jose Valencia

I often carve wildlife scenes on gunstocks, and the bison is one of my favorites. Before you try carving a gunstock, however, it's a good idea to practice on a standard blank. I recommend using harder woods with a closed grain, such as walnut, cherry, or alder, which give better results on relief carvings made with power tools.

For this project I use the Optima 2 micro motor and several bits with ⅛" (3mm)-diameter shafts. The Optima 2 Plus is a variable-speed machine with speeds that range from 8,000 to 45,000 rpm. With the dial set to 3 ½, it gives me about 13,000 rpm.

Getting Started

I use a laser printer to copy the original artwork onto special self-adhesive Mylar drafting and design appliqué film made by Chartpack. Just remove the backing paper and attach the pattern to the plate blank. You could also use ordinary Mylar or vellum and attach the pattern to the blank with spray adhesive.

1 *Outline the bison.* Use a micro cylinder-shaped high-speed steel bit to carve just outside the outline of the bison. Leave the black outline visible. Make several passes if needed to carve down ¹⁄₁₆" (2mm) to ³⁄₃₂" (2.5mm).

2 *Outline the inner details.* Using a needle-shaped diamond bit, outline the horns, eyes, nose, legs, face, and muscle structure. Cut right through the Mylar, but do not cut too deeply. Just mark the locations of the details. Use a hobby knife and stiff-bristle nylon brush to remove the stencil. Make sure the outline on the wood matches the pattern.

3 *Separate the elements.* Use a flame-shaped stump cutter to remove wood from the neck area to separate it from the front leg. Remove the wood from the legs that are farther from the viewer, from the tail, and finally from the groin. Carve the legs lower than the stomach.

4 *Carve the stomach and midsection.* Lay the stump cutter almost horizontally and take off a small amount of wood from the stomach and midsection. Use the same technique to remove wood from the midsection just above the shoulder.

5 *Round the back of the bison.* Hold the stump cutter at a 45° angle and round the edge of the bison's back from the tail to the horns. Use the same technique to round the lower portion of the stomach.

BISON: REFINING THE CARVING

6 ***Texture the legs and shoulder area.*** Lay the stump cutter almost horizontally and remove wood from the remaining legs and the shoulder area. Hold the stump cutter at a 45° angle and make random gouges on the front leg and neck area to simulate the thick and matted hair. Keep the muscle structure and movement of the hair in mind.

7 ***Refine the horns.*** Use the stump cutter to remove wood from around the horns. Remove more wood from the sides, but less wood from the base of the horns. With the stump cutter nearly flat, remove a thin layer of wood from the face. Do not "erase" the outline of the eye.

8 ***Carve the eyes, nostrils, and hooves.*** *Note: I suggest you practice rounding the eye on a piece of scrap wood before you attempt it on the project.* Using a needle-shaped diamond bit, outline the eye and then carefully round the bottom of it. Use the same bit to carve the nostrils and to separate the hooves and dewclaws.

BISON: ADDING TEXTURE

9 ***Refine the legs.*** Use a small, ball-shaped high-speed steel cutter to remove wood from between the tendons and the muscles near the hocks of the back legs. Shape the dewclaws, the rest of the hind legs, and the hooves.

10 ***Texture the face.*** Use the small ball-shaped bit to carve the face. Make light strokes in the same direction as the facial hair flow.

11 ***Carve the coarse hair.*** Use a cylinder-shaped high-speed steel bit. Hold the tool at a 45° angle and make half-circular motions to create the heavy coat of hair on the back, the front legs, and the neck. Make the hair look rough.

12 ***Carve the finer hair.*** Use a cylinder-shaped micro engraving bit. Hold the tool at a 45° angle and make short strokes to carve the shorter hair on the shoulder and neck. Make slightly longer strokes for the groin, and much longer strokes for the end of the tail.

13 ***Sand the smooth areas.*** Use sanding sticks to smooth the horns, nose, hooves, and back legs. Use the sanding sticks to sand a couple of indentations for the ribs. Then, sand the stomach and rump.

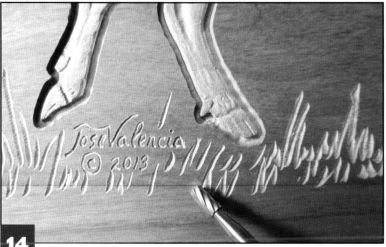

Finishing the Carving

Scrub the piece with a hard bristle brush to remove all of the dust. Apply a stain of your choice. Use an extra-fine black permanent marker to highlight the eye and the nostrils after the staining is done.

14 ***Sign the piece.*** Use a needle-shaped diamond bit to sign and date the carving. I like to blend my signature into the artwork, so I hold a cylinder-shaped high-speed steel bit at a 45° angle and make long and short strokes to represent grass around the signature and the bottom of the bison's feet.

American bison pattern

© 2013 Woodcarving Illustrated

Materials & Tools

Materials:
- Round plate, such as alder: 14" (35.6cm) diameter
- Self-adhesive Mylar drafting film, such as Chartpack, or vellum or Mylar and spray adhesive
- Stain
- Permanent marker: black extra fine

Tools:
- Rotary tool, such as an Optima 2 micro motor
- Power carving bits: micro engraver, needle-shaped diamond, flame-shaped stump cutter, high-speed steel micro cylinder-shaped, high-speed steel cylinder shaped, high-speed steel ball-shaped
- Sanding sticks in assorted grits
- Hobby knife
- Stiff-bristle nylon brush

The author used these products for the project.
Substitute your choice of brands, tools, and materials as desired.

Jose Valencia Gunstock Carvings

A Benelli shotgun with a dog and pheasant carving.

Whitetail deer gunstock carving.

A Winchester '73 with a Native American-themed carving.

Santa Caricature

By Frank Russell

This Santa was carved as a mantel decoration (the original was about 14", or 35.6cm, tall). It is dedicated to all of us who have experienced the joy of eating the cookies and milk left out by loving (and expectant!) little hands.

The mittens—one with a glass of milk, the other with a chocolate chip cookie—are more easily carved separately, and then inserted into the sleeves of the coat, allowing for greater detail around and behind the mittens, milk, cookie, and furred sleeve edges.

Materials & Tools

Materials:
- Wood of choice
- Acrylic paints—see color chart on page 89
- 5-minute epoxy

Tools:
- Band saw or scroll saw
- Carbide bits: small flame-shaped, medium flame-shaped
- Ruby bits: small flame-shaped, medium flame-shaped, safe-end long taper, small bud-shaped
- Diamond bit: very small ball-shaped, small inverted cone, medium inverted come, small long flame-shaped, small narrow flame-shaped
- Stone bit: small cylinder-shaped
- Defuzzing mandrel or rotary bristle brush

SANTA: CUTTING THE BLANK

1 ***Saw the project on the bandsaw.*** Draw a vertical centerline all the way around the blank. A centerline is necessary to maintain symmetry during and throughout the carving sequences.

2 ***Lay out all areas to be wasted away or rough shaped.*** Use a small and medium flame-shaped carbide bur and a medium flame-shaped ruby carver.

SANTA: ROUGHING CUT

3 ***Rough shape areas of clothing, such as the hat, coat, trousers, and boots.*** Rough shape areas with hair, such as the beard, mustache, head hair, and fur trim on clothing. Use a safe-end long-taper ruby carver and small and medium flame-shaped ruby carvers.

4 ***Lay out and detail the clothing—the wrinkles, creases, folds, belt, belt buckle, and buttons.*** Use small and medium flame-shaped ruby carvers.

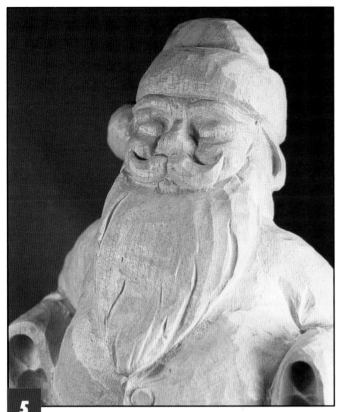

5 ***Lay out and shape the contours of the face.*** Do the nose, eye mounds, cheeks, eyebrows, and wrinkles. Use small flame- and bud-shaped ruby carvers.

6 ***Detail the face.*** Do the eyes and nose/nostrils and give a final touch to the wrinkles. Use the small flame-shaped ruby carver and a very small ball-shaped diamond bit.

7 ***Texture all areas of hair or fur.*** Use a small cylinder-shaped stone bit for eyebrows. Then use small and medium inverted cone-shaped diamond bits and a small, long flame-shaped diamond bit for drag strokes into hair where it meets the face. Clean and defuzz the carving with a rotary bristle brush.

8 ***Texture the tassel.*** The tassel was textured by plunging a small, narrow flame-shaped diamond bit to various depths at 90° to the surface over entire tassel.

BEGINNER

9 *Lay out and rough shape the mittens.* Both mittens were carved separately from the body and blanked out on the ends of longer pieces of stock to provide a handle for ease of carving. Use small and medium flame-shaped ruby carvers.

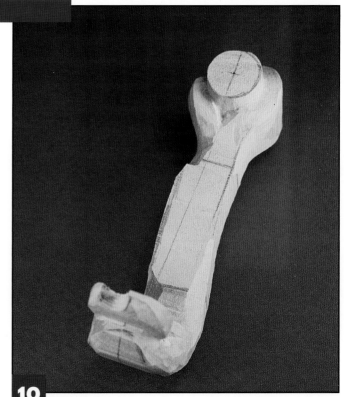

10 *Finish shape the mittens, cookie, and milk.* Use a small flame-shaped ruby carver.

11 *Detail the mittens, cookie, and milk.* Create wrinkles and do the crumbs/chips on the cookie. Finish the depth of milk in the glass with the safe-end tapered ruby carver. Use the small flame-shaped ruby carver elsewhere.

12 *Texture the mittens with a knit stitch.* The stitch effect is accomplished by laying out the direction of the knitting with pencil, and then touching a small inverted diamond bit to the surface in opposing rows of 45° angles, which come together to form a 90° V. Clean and defuzz the mittens with a rotary bristle brush.

Color Chart for Santa Caricature

Trousers, coat, and hat base coat: Grumbacher red

Trousers, coat, and hat shadows: burnt umber

Trousers, coat, and hat highlights: cadmium red light

Fur trim, tassel base coat: Mars black, raw umber, and titanium white mixed to make a medium gray

Fur trim, tassel highlight: titanium white

Boots, belt base coat: Mars black and raw umber

Boots, belt highlight: titanium white

Belt buckle base: metallic gold

Belt buckle shadow: wet blend in burnt sienna on edges

Face, exposed flesh base: cadmium red medium, cadmium yellow medium, and titanium white mixed to a flesh tone

Face, exposed flesh shadow: burnt umber

Rosy cheeks and nose: cadmium red medium

Eye whites, highlight dot: titanium white with a touch of raw umber

Iris: ultramarine blue toned down with titanium white and a touch of raw umber

Pupil: Mars black and raw umber

Hair, eyebrows, beard, mustache base and shadow: Payne's grey lightened with titanium white

Hair, eyebrows, beard, mustache highlight: titanium white

Cookie base coat: burnt sienna, burnt umber, and a touch of titanium white

Cookie shadow: raw umber

Milk base coat: titanium white with a touch of rad umber

Milk glass: thin wash of ultramarine blue

Mittens base coat: Grumbacher red

Mittens shadow: burnt umber

Mittens highlights: cadmium red light

(Use 5-minute epoxy to attach mittens to the sleeves after the paint dries)

Antiquing coat over entire piece: Thin raw umber with water to create a wash

Santa caricature pattern

Photocopy to desired size

Contemporary Primitive Loon Decoy

By Frank Russell

For years I made Contemporary Primitives for home and workplace decoration. At one point, I was carving 32 different shorebirds, waders, and waterfowl with virtually no time for anything else.

One of the more important aspects to carving a primitive is the antiquing process which makes the carving look old, used, and aged. To make them look authentic, I actually took many of my decoy reproductions out in a field and shot at them from a distance with number 6 shot to make them look as though they had been shot over (and into) on the water.

Contemporary primitive is a term I applied to them because I wanted folks to know that they were made by modern means but using old shapes and painting patterns. Some folks actually believe them to be antiques until I explain that they were made a week ago!

Materials & Tools

Materials:
- Wood of choice
- Screw, eyebolt, and waterproof glue
- Glass eye (optional)
- Paints and sealer
- Glass enamel or lacquer
- Raw umber acrylic paint for antiquing wash (optional)
- Paste furniture polish with color and soft cloth

Tools:
- Band saw or scroll saw
- Carbide bits: small flame-shaped, medium flame-shaped
- Ruby carvers: medium flame-shaped, large flame-shaped, medium bud-shaped
- Sanding mandrels: 1" and ½" (25mm and 13mm) with 200-grit paper and defuzzing
- Propane torch
- Coarse and fine steel wool and coarse cloth

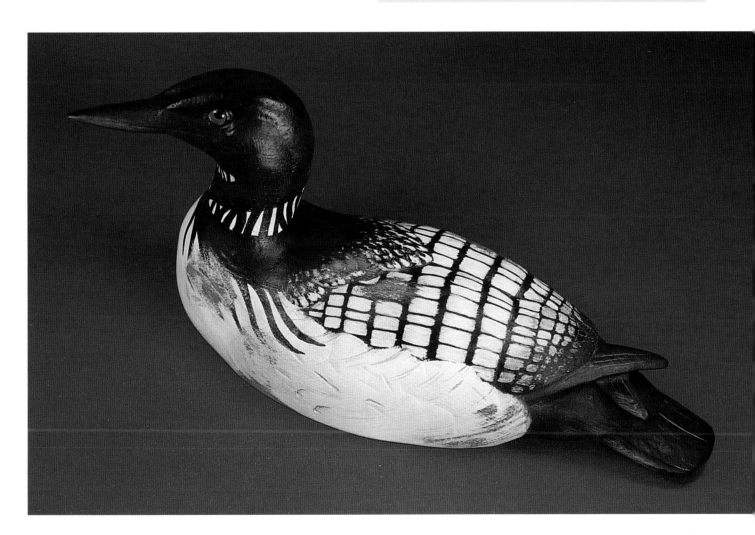

LOON DECOY: ROUGHING OUT

1 **_Blank out the body and head separately._** Draw a vertical centerline completely around each piece. Carve the head separate from the body—a piece is unwieldy while carving the head with a body attached or vice-versa.

2 **_Rough shape the head and body._** Use small and medium flame-shaped carbide burs.

LOON DECOY: DEFINING THE FEATHER GROUPS

3 **_Lay out and shape major feather group areas on the body._** Do the cape, side pockets, breast, back, wing coverts, wings, tail coverts, and tail. Lay out and shape contours of the head—bill, jowls, cheeks (auricular area), eye holes, top of head, and neck. For decorative purposes, I use glass eyes. For gunning purposes, I usually carve the eyes because extreme temperatures, moisture, and hard use often cause glass eyes to loosen and the wood or filler material around them to crack. Use medium and large flame-shaped ruby carvers.

4 **_Join the head to the body in the desired position and glue._** I usually run a long screw up through a predrilled and countersunk hole through the body into the head because it acts as a clamp while the waterproof glue dries. For a working decoy, an eyebolt for the anchor line through the keel, body, and into the head serves the same purpose.

5 **_Smooth out the carving._** Smooth out the body/head joint and the body and head, and lay out a few representative feathers in conspicuous areas along the back and sides. Shape and smooth all feathered areas. Use medium flame-shaped and medium bud-shaped ruby carvers and 1" and ½" (25mm and 13mm) sanding mandrels with 200-grit paper. Defuzz with a defuzzing mandrel.

6 ***Char the decoy.*** Using a propane torch, burn random locations around the head and body to different degrees. Avoid glue joints! Clean the decoy with fine steel wool or a large defuzzing mandrel and wipe off residue with a coarse cloth.

7 ***Install the eyes if glass eyes are to be used.*** Then, seal and paint as desired. For a "primitive," the old Bayman style of painting without a great amount of fine feather detail is used—just representative color patterns, so that "a mallard looks like a mallard" at a distance. There is very little blending, highlighting, shading, or feather detailing. If eyes are carved, paint them the desired color (red for a loon, with a black pupil), and coat them with several coats of glass enamel or lacquer.

8 ***Distress or age the painted piece with coarse steel wool in random locations.*** Don't overdo it. Dents can be added (optional) with a blunt edge implement like a pipe, a solid rod, or even the edge of a rounded bench. Add whatever scratches or dents you desire, depending on how used or aged you want the piece to look. This is also a good way to hide some painting flaws! Stay away from the eyes at all times.

9 ***Flow an antiquing fluid over the entire piece.*** Allow the fluid to lie in indentations, feather group separations, scratches, and dents. Wipe off high areas and dry the decoy with a hair dryer if you are using acrylic paints. I make an antiquing fluid by mixing raw umber with lots of water. You want an earth color that looks like the dirt and grime that accumulates with age and misuse. Repeat with washes until the desired antiquing color depth is acquired. Allow it to dry completely.

10 ***Apply a generous coat of paste furniture polish with color.*** Allow it to dry; then, vigorously buff the high points, leaving the indentations and low areas dull. I use an old athletic sock to polish. By keeping my fingers stiff, I can avoid polishing the low areas and buff only the high areas.

Loon decoy pattern

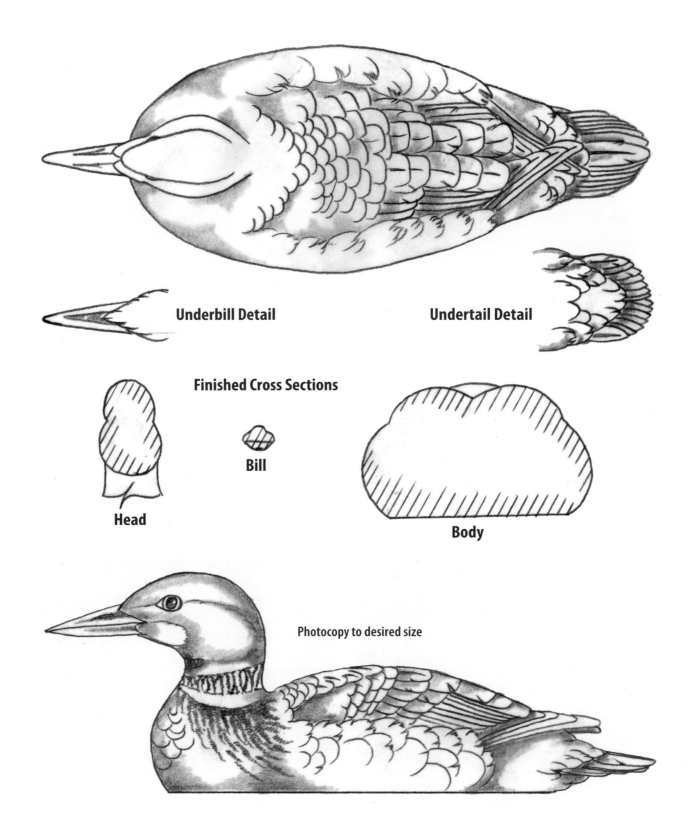

Underbill Detail

Undertail Detail

Finished Cross Sections

Head

Bill

Body

Photocopy to desired size

Maple Leaf Earrings

By Kenny Vermillion
Photography by Carl Saathoff

Not every carving has to be a complicated composition. This is a wonderful exercise for developing both power carving and painting skills. Learning new techniques can be discouraging if projects take forever to complete. Small items such as these are challenging, due to their size, while being achievable in a relatively short period of time. These earrings are also attractive and a popular sale or gift item.

Almost everything I carve is from tupelo because it has ideal qualities for wildlife subjects. These maple leaf earrings are made of scrap wood from other subjects. I have always used acrylic paint. Most of my students are intimidated by painting, but once they understand a logical approach, they usually enjoy it.

EARRINGS: GETTING STARTED

1 ***Cut the blank to shape.*** The blank is sawn from a select piece of wood with flat grain running from front to back with the center vein. The blank is cut in half to create two symmetrical earrings. After sawing, lightly sand the back of each leaf with fine-grit sandpaper. Draw on the leaf vein details. I use a mechanical pencil with 0.5mm HB lead. Draw lightly, because you cannot erase scribing. Curved veins are more natural and pleasing to the eye.

2 ***Establish the veins with the small, pointed diamond bit.*** Create shallow furrows by pulling the bit the full length of the veins. Point the bit to the center of the leaf and lightly pull toward the outside edge for better control. Do not use pressure or force the tool—merely guide the bit.

3 *Carve the remainder of the leaf top with the small flame diamond bit.* Begin to deepen and contour the veins. The center vein is shallowest in the center and deepens at each end. The side veins originate from the center vein. Gently lead the bit, execute the stroke, and follow through. Flicking creates dips instead of contours. Short strokes are easier to control than long ones. Understand where you are going before carving.

4 *Follow the rotation of the tool when carving.* Avoid stroking over the edge of the leaf that is farthest away because it will dig and run over the side. Rotate the leaf when carving on the edge. This will facilitate stroking forward from the outside toward the center. The grain will dictate whether you should orient the bit straight or diagonally.

5 *Contour the leaf by creating sweeping peaks and valleys.* Use the side of the bit and lightly stroke in the direction of the bit rotation. Pulling against the rotation sacrifices control. The outside edges are deeper in the veins and higher between them. Retain enough thickness to ensure the strength of the leaf. The veins are well-defined in the center of the leaf, and more varied toward the edges. Still using the side of the bit, it may be necessary to stroke diagonally across the grain of the wood to remove it evenly.

6 *Reduce the grit of a bonded ruby bit.* Ruby bits tend to be coarse and inconsistent. Run the bit at high speed and carefully brush it across a diamond strop. It is important to reduce the grit consistently from the hilt to the point. Frequently run the side of the bit on a scrap piece of wood to test for spikes and inconsistencies. Be careful not to remove all of the grit.

7 *Redefine the veins.* Use the reduced-grit bonded ruby bit and slowly pull the point from the center toward the edge at a high rpm. Smooth each section between the veins. Stroking diagonally across the grain will smooth it evenly.

8 *Reduce the diameter of the ruby stone.* Stroke the side on a diamond strop at moderate rpms. Use the bonding agent at the base of the stone as a guide. Do not remove the stone all the way to the shaft. Be careful—if the stone gets too hot, the bonding agent will break down and the stone will be worthless.

9 *Lightly soften the saw marks.* Use the side of the reduced-diameter ruby stone at a high rpm around the sides of the leaf. Hold the stone parallel to the saw marks and stroke carefully to maintain them evenly up and down the sides. Use the side of the tip of the ruby stone at a moderate rpm to lightly round the edges on both top and bottom on all sides of the leaf. Wooden 90° angles on edges chip and break.

EARRINGS: ATTACHING THE POST

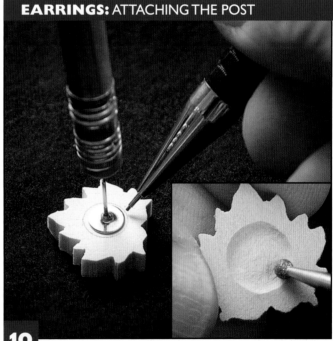

10 *Carve a recess to accommodate the earring posts.* Center the post on the back of the earring. Hold it in place with a pencil eraser, and trace the outline with a pencil. Follow the pencil line using a small diamond ball to recess the wood the approximate thickness of the post base. Clean out the recess using slow, forward strokes for consistent depth. A flat bottom is important for the post to set squarely.

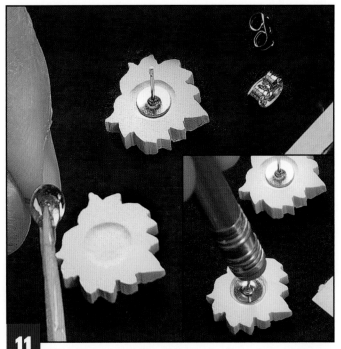

11 *Glue the post onto the earring using five-minute epoxy.* Mix the epoxy according to the manufacturer's directions. Apply it the bottom of the post bases with a toothpick. If it strings from the toothpick, it has already begun to set up and should not be used. Use the pencil eraser to press the post base into the recess. Then, use a pencil to put your initials on the backs.

12 *Make clamps to hold the earrings.* Use five-minute epoxy to glue a notched dowel to the outside of a clothespin. Cut a popsicle stick in half and glue it to the inside of the clothespin. This gives you something to hold on to when painting. The dowels can be inserted into holes drilled in a scrap 2x4 to hold the clamps while the paint dries.

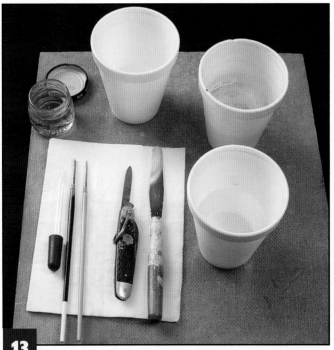

13 *Organize your painting supplies.* Set up three cups of water. One cup of water (the upper left) is for mixing with paint and must be kept clean. The other two are used to clean brushes—always do the first swishing of the brush in the same cup and the final swishing in the other. The window cleaner with ammonia in the jar is used to clean the brushes (see Cleaning Up Paintbrushes on page 101). The eyedropper is used to measure out water, and the knife and spatula are used to measure paints (see Step 15). The stiff-bristled brush is used to mix the paints, and the camel hair brush is used to apply the paint.

14 *Apply a spray lacquer.* The wood must be well-sealed to prevent the grain from rising. Apply three or four light coats to the top, sides, and bottom. Let the lacquered earrings set for at least 12 hours before painting, then peel the lacquer off of the post. Mix a few drops of white gesso with water to the consistency of milk and apply a very small amount to the tip of the camel hair brush. Wipe one side on the edge of the palette well. Paint from the center vein out, one section at a time, with as few strokes as possible. Apply the gesso to the top of the leaf only. Apply a second coat after the first coat has thoroughly dried. Even coverage is necessary.

15 ***Measure out a small amount of paint.*** Use an old knife to scrape a small amount from the end of the tube. Wipe this paint on the side of the palette well and use the eyedropper to add a few drops of water. Dip the stiff-bristled brush in water and then mix the paint. Add water as needed to get the consistency of skim milk.

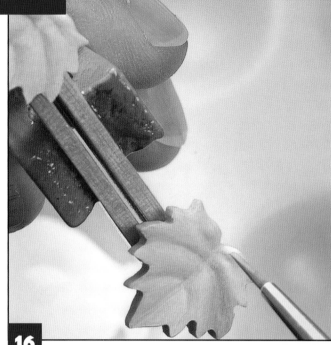

16 ***Apply an even coat of yellow to the top of the leaf.*** Use the camel hair brush and the same techniques you used to apply the Gesso. This is a base color coat because the paint is translucent. If one coat does not cover evenly, apply additional coats as needed. Allow each coat to dry before adding the next. To keep the paint for future use, cover the palette with a wet sponge.

Tips:

REMOVING FOREIGN MATERIAL

If you have a speck of foreign material on the surface, lift it off with the brush you are using. However, if this doesn't work, the dull knife will. Be careful to not dig into the previous coats.

RETOUCHING

Resist the temptation to retouch before the paint has dried. The paint is continually drying, so if strokes are repeatedly overlapped, the latest stroke will lift the paint from the first strokes.

TOUCH-UPS

Touch-ups can be done by touching the brush tip to the paint and then stippling or dabbing onto the leaf.

STEADY HANDS

Brace your hands together when carving the earring. Since it is so small, it is easiest to hold the earring in your hand, but even normal breathing makes it hard to hold your hands steady. Hold the power carver the same as a pencil and extend one finger to touch the hand holding the earring. That way, if your hands move, they are more likely to move together—giving you coordinated control.

17 ***Mix equal amounts of the yellow and red with water to get orange.*** Use a separate palette well. Brush one coat onto the veins. This is the beginning of the build-up of color. Blending acrylic paints with only one coat is very difficult. More pleasing results are achieved with multiple thin coats that overlap or underlap. Each coat must be dry before applying the next.

18 ***Swish and wipe your brush.*** Touch the tip of the brush to the orange paint. Starting on the first section of the leaf, touch the point of the brush to the outside edge, next to the center vein. Hold the brush slightly on its side with the ferrule toward the section's vein, and stroke along the outside perimeter of the section. Paint each remaining section of the leaf in the same manner. The perimeters of each section should be orange and the centers should be yellow. Save this color for future use.

19 ***Mix red paint with water.*** Mix the same quantity as you did with the yellow (in Step 15). Stir both the red and yellow paint as both will be used. Touch the tip of the brush to the red, and paint the perimeter of the first section. Quickly wipe the brush on a paper towel, touch the tip of the brush to the yellow, and paint the center of this same section. Gently stroke where the red and yellow meet. Do not overwork it; two or three strokes should be enough. The leaf on the right shows the first coat of orange and the leaf on the left shows the red and yellow blending.

EARRINGS: FINISHING

20 *Return to the orange color.* Increase the volume by one-third with water, and stir well. This will be the homogenizing wash that ties all of the colors together. One coat should be enough. Mix burnt sienna, a very small amount of acra violet, and a couple drops of water to a consistency of thick cream. Using vertical strokes (follow the saw marks), paint the sides with this color all the way around the leaf. Too much pressure on the brush will squeeze paint onto the top and bottom of the leaf.

21 *Mix the gloss medium and varnish with water to the consistency of milk.* Put one coat on the top. Be careful not to get it on the sides. This establishes two finishes which adds visual interest. Put the backs on the posts to complete the earrings.

Materials & Tools

Materials:
- Tupelo, ⅜" (1cm) thick: 1" (2.5cm) square
- 5-minute epoxy glue
- Earring posts and backs
- Acrylic tube paints: brilliant yellow, cadmium red light, burnt sienna, acra violet
- Interior/exterior spray lacquer
- Gesso
- Gloss medium and varnish

Tools:
- Band saw or scroll saw
- Diamond strop (medium or fine grit)
- Diamond bits (medium grit): small point, small flame-shaped, small ball-shaped
- Bonded ruby bit: small flame-shaped, fine grit
- Ruby stone bit, tapered
- Stiff-bristled brush
- Camel hair brush

Tips:

CLEANING UP PAINTBRUSHES

Ammonia is a solvent for acrylic paint and window cleaner with ammonia contains just the right amount. Occasional swishing of the brushes in window cleaner prolongs their life by cleaning the paint from the ferrules. When paint dries in the brush ferrule, the bristles splay and become brittle. Follow swishing in the window cleaner by swishing in both water cups then dragging off on the towel to complete the procedure.

Enlarge the pattern for clip-on earrings.

Photocopy at 100%

Maple leaf earring pattern

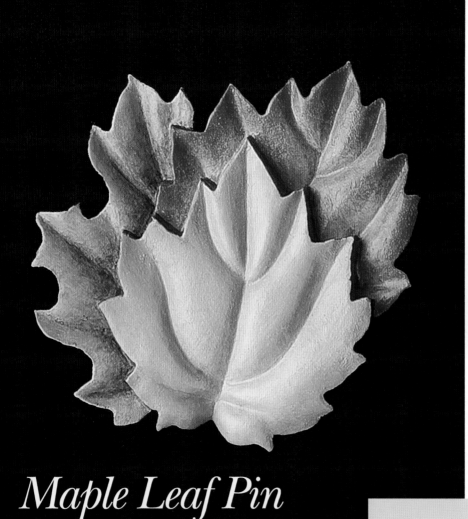

This delightful fall accent can be work alone, or paired with the leaf earrings. The pin uses the same techniques used to create the earrings, but is more challenging due to the multiple layers.

I use tupelo for this piece, but you can use your wood and tools of choice. The pattern is provided, but it's important to keep in mind that a pattern is intended to be interpreted—not followed like a blueprint. Feel free to alter the pattern, experiment with different techniques, or change the colors.

Maple Leaf Pin

By Kenny Vermillion
Photography by Carl Saathoff

Maple leaf pin pattern

Photocopy at 100%

Materials & Tools

Materials:

- Tupelo, ⅜" (1cm) thick: 2" (5.1cm) square
- Pin back
- 5-minute epoxy
- Toothpick (to mix epoxy)
- Wet sponge (to keep paint in palette from drying out)
- Window cleaner with ammonia (to clean brushes)
- Palette
- White gesso
- Acrylic tube paints: brilliant yellow, cadmium red light, cadmium red medium, Hookers green, burnt sienna, acra violet

Tools:

- Power carver of choice
- Mechanical pencil with .5mm HB lead
- Sandpaper, 220 grit
- Diamond bur: large flame-shaped, small flame-shaped
- Stump cutter: cylinder, egg-shaped
- Reduced-grit, bonded ruby bur
- Fine-grit diamond hone
- Aluminum oxide stone: ball-shaped
- Reduced-diameter ruby stone
- Old carving knife (to measure paint)
- Paintbrushes: at least one stiff-bristled brush to mix with, and a camel hair brush to apply the paint

Carve and Paint a Killdeer

By Jack Kochan

You don't have to be a professional wildfowl carver to capture the essence of an attractive shorebird like the killdeer. In the traditions of nineteenth- and early twentieth-century decoy makers who lured birds to marshes and beaches with counterfeits, the carved bird can be approached as a simple but pleasing form, shaped, sanded, and finished with nothing more than a dark shoe polish. Mount it on a stick as the old timers did, and the killdeer lends itself handsomely to a mantel or shelf instead of a shoreline.

My finished piece isn't quite so simple, but the techniques needed to bring more realism to the killdeer are not hard to master and power carving makes it all that much easier. After rounding its body, I shaped the eyes, ground in the wing outlines, turned the head, and settled for a paint application that brings out the basic colors of the bird plus a few feather details.

Tupelo, a Power Carver's First Choice

While the decoy makers of a bygone era used cedar or pine to fashion their birds, I prefer tupelo for several reasons. Being a power carver, I find tupelo and rotary tools are natural allies. Chips and dust come away from a cutout with little resistance. Because of the seemingly grainless nature of the wood—actually, it's an interlocking grain—fuzzy surfaces are not a problem. Basswood and jelutong also lend themselves to power carving, but they require a lot of extra sanding to remove wood fibers that tend to stick up like tiny hairs.

Be advised: tupelo does not carve easily with hand tools. Cutting edges rely on grain direction and firmness to slice and even make stop cuts. Knives, chisels, and gouges meet a lot of resistance with tupelo's grain, and consequently the wood is often described as spongy in texture. However, tupelo has no hard and soft transitions between growth rings, unlike pine.

In my mind, the biggest advantage to using tupelo is that thin pieces resist breakage. Because of the interlocking grain, there is strength in all directions. A fragile area like the bill of the killdeer, while not completely safe from damage, won't cause as much concern as a bill carved from basswood.

Tupelo, however, is a thirsty wood that will soak up the humidity in your carving area and cause the wood to swell.

By the next morning, you may well find that the fine burning and stoning lines have lost their crispness. Sealing the wood with a thin coat of lacquer prior to turning in for the night remedies that problem.

Primed for Painting

Before opening up the paint containers or purchasing colors, take some time to study my painting notes. I sealed the bird prior to painting and applied several coats of gesso that I mixed with a flow medium. An acrylic additive, the flow medium modifies the handling properties of the paint and allows for smoother application. The gesso mix actually lends itself to one of the primary colors of the killdeer. Additional applications were required to cover the filler used at the neck joint. The rest of the colors were acrylic gouaches.

Many wildfowl carvers use gouaches because of their flat, non-glossy finish, which more closely resembles a feather's lifelike sheen. Having pigments that are more finely ground than other paints, the gouaches lend themselves well to airbrushing, and they do not fill in fine texturing details when several thin washes are applied.

I could have simplified the painting by limiting the bird to two color tones, one for the belly and the other for the head, back, and tail. But I opted to paint individual feathers on the cape and primaries, dark stripes on the breast and forehead, and a white stripe above the eyes. I even gave some color to the eyes to make them more realistic.

When mounted on a wood base, in this case a cross section of a limb from my fireplace woodpile, the killdeer is an attention getter even when viewed up close.

Killdeer pattern

Photocopy at 100%

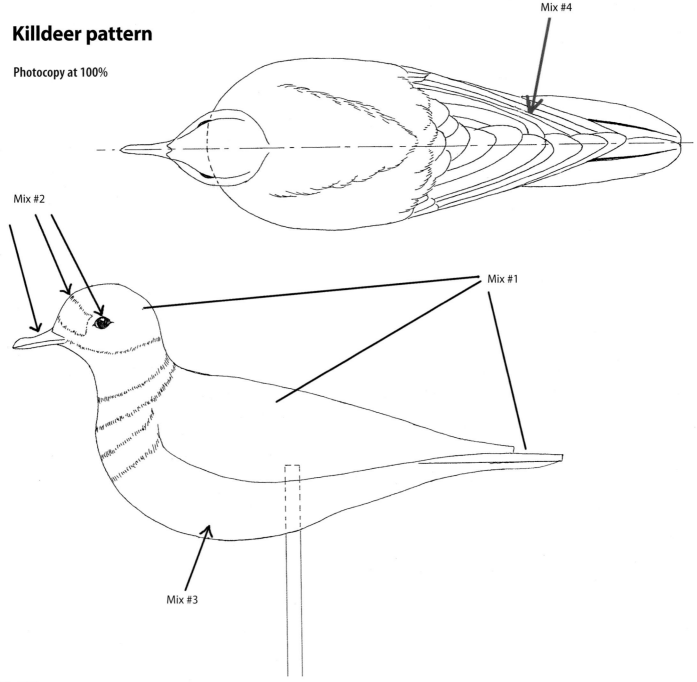

Mix #4

Mix #2

Mix #1

Mix #3

1 ***Cut the block.*** Photocopy the side pattern and glue it directly to the wood. Select a piece of wood larger and thicker than the pattern to give the bandsaw blade extra room to maneuver and to keep your fingers a safe distance from the cutting edge.

2 ***Mark.*** Draw a centerline on both the top and bottom of the cutout.

3 ***Draw the width of the head and mark off the waste wood.*** Keep it blockish at this stage. Leave extra wood on the bill because it is a fragile area and you do not want it too narrow at this stage.

4 ***By tilting the cutout, remove the waste wood on the head with the bandsaw.*** Use a piece of the wood sawn away from the side profile as a supportive cradle.

5 ***Cut the top profile.*** Glue the top profile on the wood and cut it out on the bandsaw. Cradle the cutout with a piece of wood sawn from the side profile.

6 ***Mark the wings and tail.*** After the top profile is cut to shape, mark the thickness of the wings and determine how much wood needs to be removed to separate them from the tail. Make sure that the tail remains straight from front to back, a natural characteristic of all birds.

7 ***Cut the wings and tail.*** Block out the wing and tail separation using a cylindrical diamond bit in a rotary tool. Remove wood using the outline of the wing tip profile as a guide.

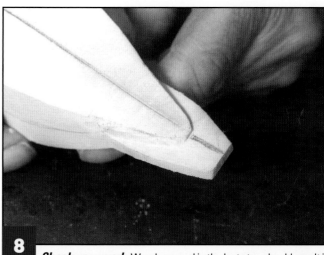

8 ***Check your work.*** Wood removal in the last step should result in a layered or stepped look. The tip of the wing feathers should be a maximum of ⅛" (3mm) thick.

9 ***Work the undertail coverts.*** Turn the bird over and mark off the undertail covert area. Remove waste wood using the cylindrical diamond bit, leaving about ⅛" to 3/16" (3mm to 5mm) of wood. If you are aiming for realism, make the tail slightly concave on its underside.

10 ***Draw the profile of the wings and mark the widest point of the cutout on both sides.*** When rounding the body in the next step, work from the top and bottom centerlines toward those marks.

KILLDEER: SHAPING THE BODY

11 ***Round the body.*** Use a medium-grade ball nose carbide bur.

12 ***Round the breast area.*** You want as perfect a circle as you can achieve. Make a cardboard template with a half circle removed from it as a guide if you have trouble visualizing the front profile. Once the breast is rounded, work toward the rear of the bird.

13 ***Smooth out the bird.*** Burs leave rough grinding marks on the wood. Use the cylindrical diamond bit to smooth the wood as much as possible. Hand sanding also removes coarse marks left by the burs. A cloth-backed sandpaper is a good choice.

14 ***Define the wings.*** The front of the wings starts at the widest part of the bird. After penciling in the wing lines, relieve each wing along its bottom edge with the cylindrical diamond bit. The difference in width between a wing and body should be about 1/16" (2mm).

KILLDEER: CARVING THE HEAD

15 ***Mark the head.*** Pencil in the outline of the head, using the pattern as reference. The eyes are located at the widest part of the head.

16 ***Mark the wood to be removed.*** The sides of the head need to be reduced in thickness. However, don't take as much wood away in the cheek areas, which are fuller. Make sure to mark the location of the eyes.

17 ***Carve the head.*** Remove wood on the head with the carbide cutter used for rounding the body. Do not shape the bill yet.

18 ***Use a round-nosed stump cutter to finish rounding the head.*** The head is egg-shaped, tapered in the front and slightly flat on top. Bring the bill to its final width, making sure to keep it in a straight line with the head. Protect the bill by saturating it with cyanoacrylate (CA) glue.

19 *Punch the eyes.* A piece of brass tubing with a wooden handle makes a perfect eye punch. A moderate pressure is required to set the eyes in. If you prefer glass eyes, drill holes and set them in with epoxy putty.

20 *Mark the head for cutting.* The killdeer looks more animated if the head is turned slightly. It is easier to cut the head off and turn it now than it is to carve the head in a turned position. A pencil held at a set height makes for an ideal marking tool. Use a fine handsaw to cut off the head.

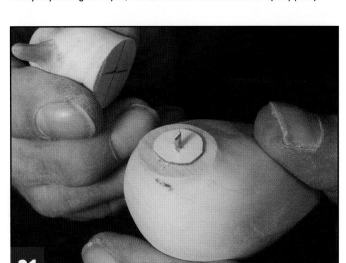

21 *Re-attach the head and body with a short piece of copper wire.* To make up for the saw kerf or thickness, set a piece of cardboard or a thin slice of tupelo on the body to raise the head slightly. Apoxie® Sculpt is a good filler to cover the gap.

22 *Round the eyes and complete the bill.* Use a flame-shaped blue stone to round the eyes and finish shape the bill.

23 *Detail the wing feathers.* For a pleasing finishing touch, delineate the wing feathers using a cylindrical white stone. A burning pen can also be used.

KILLDEER: FINISHING

24 *Finish.* The final sanding prior to painting is accomplished by using a variety of grits, ranging from 100 to 400. After sanding, select a suitable base and drill holes for the dowel in both the bird and the base. Use a hand drill because it is easier to control the angle of penetration.

Painting and Finishing Tips

PREP:

1. Sand the completed carving with cloth-backed sandpaper, starting with 120-grit, then 220-grit, then 400-grit sandpaper.

2. Seal with a 50/50 mix of lacquer and lacquer thinner. Let it dry for a minimum of four hours, then lightly sand with 400-grit sandpaper.

3. Mix gesso and 25% flow medium; brush over the entire carving. Dry with a hair dryer, then sand and apply a second coat of gesso mix. Repeat until evenly white, and set aside for 24 hours to dry.

4. Remove any fuzz on the carving by scrubbing with a clean, dry toothbrush or 400-grit sandpaper.

PAINT:

1. Use a watercolor pencil to sketch the locations of stripes on the breast, forehead, and above the eyes.

2. For the head, back, and tail, use Mix #1 (refer to swatches), add a few drops of flow medium, and apply as illustrated with a #8 filbert brush. Repeat until the desired color is achieved.

3. For the black stripes, the eyes, and bill, use Mix #2; add a few drops of flow medium and apply as illustrated. Build up coats until a dark black is achieved; drag a little black onto the white areas to give the appearance of feather overlap.

4. After the eyes are dry, paint eyelids with naphthol red.

5. For the bird's underside, use Mix #3 and paint over all the white areas. Use the same mix to paint a narrow stripe over each eye.

6. Use Mix #4 and paint the primary wing feather tips using a small liner brush.

7. Let it dry for at least eight hours.

FINISH:

1. Spray the piece with a semi-gloss acrylic varnish; let it dry for at least 24 hours.

2. For an antique look, apply brown wax shoe polish to the entire surface with a soft cloth. Apply lightly over the white areas and buff with a clean, soft cloth to bring out a glow.

3. Spray several coats of clear varnish on the base and dowel.

4. Glue the dowel to the bird, and attach it to the base.

MIX #1

MIX #2

MIX #3

MIX #4

Materials & Tools

Wood
- Tupelo, 2" (5.1cm) thick: 3" x 6" (7.6cm x 15.2cm)
- Hardwood dowel, ¼" (6mm)-diameter
- Scrap wood or tree limb cross section

Tools
- Rotary tools: flexible shaft machine, micro motor
- Carbide cutter: medium-grade ball-nosed
- Diamond bit: cylindrical
- Stump cutter: round nosed
- Blue stone: flame-shaped
- White stone: cylindrical
- Brass tubing: ⁵⁄₃₂" (4mm)-diameter
- Fine handsaw

Finishing Materials
- Cyanoacrylate (CA) glue
- Cloth-backed sandpaper
- Copper wire: 12 or 14 gauge
- Apoxie Sculpt
- Gesso
- Flow medium
- Acrylic paints

Carving Habitat: Twig

By Kenny Vermillion
Photography by Carl Saathoff

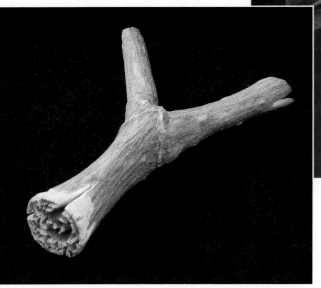

Above: A real twig can be the wrong size for a carving. But if you carve one, you can size it to the carving.
Above right: A similar twig used as a habitat element.

Tips on Hand Holding

The twig should always be handheld while carving. Normal breathing causes the hands to independently move uncontrollably. Hold the power carver the same as a pencil, and extend a finger from one hand to touch the other. Now when one hand moves, the other moves with it for coordinated control.

Take a look at the top winners in any bird or wildlife carving competition, and you'll notice many have a common element—a detailed habitat designed to highlight the main subject. You could use actual elements from nature, but they are often the wrong scale and can detract from your overall carving rather than enhance it. By carving your own habitat, you can achieve the specific effect you are striving for and create a professional presentation for your carving.

Examine short sections of a real twig and take note of the interesting details. Figure out how to replicate some of these details on your twig. The variety of colors found in a natural stick make me think of impressionism, and that has influenced how I paint some subjects.

Choose a real, single-forked twig for reference. Carving is a process. First, determine the details you want to incorporate in your own carving and sketch them on the twig. Remove the wood around the details, then break each detail area down into components. When approached in chunks like this, even the most complicated carving becomes achievable. Analyze the colors in the same manner. Gesso the entire carving to prepare the surface for color details. Identify specific areas and the appropriate color. Systematically build cumulative coats of paint to the desired depth of color and finish.

Approach carving and painting as a refining process. From the first cut, it is correcting the shape to conform to the pattern, and from the first coat of gesso it is about correcting the colors. From start to finish, it is a series of corrections.

TWIG: ROUGHING OUT

1 *Rough out the twig.* Divide each side into three equal sections. These lines are important references. Without them, it is easy to remove too much wood, creating a flat or undesired radius. Use a pear-shaped stump cutter to remove the original four corners to the pencil lines to create an octagon. Hold the bit at an oblique angle and carve from the ends toward the center. Round the twig by lightly stroking the bit along it.

2 *Rough out the details.* Draw details, such as fissures and buds on the sides. Use a real twig as a reference. Remove wood around each pencil line with a small ball-shaped diamond bur, being careful not to cut too deep. Evenly relieve the wood between the details. Stroke forward because pulling against the rotation creates digs. Use this diamond ball to make the texture and grooves of the bark between and around the details.

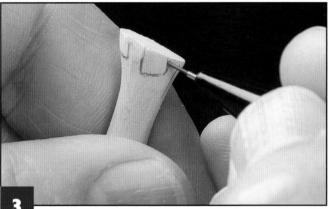

3 *Draw the details on the ends of the twig.* When a stick is broken, the bark tears unevenly exposing the cambium. The cambium is the layer of tissue below the bark sometimes referred to as the second layer of bark. Sketch some of these tears. When drawing and carving on any project, rather than "grip" the piece, "hold" it. Gripping can cause writer's cramp and, over time, tendonitis.

4 *Rough in the splits and breaks.* Consider the circular growth rings when sketching the splits. Use a tapered-point diamond bur to make the large splits. Increase the depth with each pass. Jamming the bur in will burn the wood. Refer to a real twig to determine cut depth. Use a cylinder-shaped stump cutter to cut the next largest splits. Ease the bit straight into the end of the twig, as a drill bit, and move it sideways to define some splits.

TWIG: DETAILING THE ENDS

5 *Relieve the wood from the perimeter of the ends.* Use a tapered stump cutter. There are two layers of bark, and when broken, they sometimes separate and only one is torn off. Notice that these tears may be quite shallow, ragged, and of various lengths.

6 *Continue detailing the ends.* With the tapered stump cutter, etch small splits within the designated areas on the perimeter of each end. Stay with the tapered stump cutter to carve even smaller splits in the twig ends. Continue following the dictates of the growth rings.

7 ***Refine, deepen, and taper the splits.*** Use a pointed diamond bur. Use this bit in the same fashion as in Step 4 (like a drill bit). Too much force can break the tip of the bit. This creates even smaller splits and splinters. Lightly buff the splits to remove the fuzz and fragments with the pointed stone. The buffing also rounds the brittle edges to give a time-worn appearance. This stone can also define other features on the twig.

8 ***Clean up the texture and grooves of the bark.*** Use a round stone to clean up the cuts made by the ball-shaped diamond bit. Refine any detail marks at this time and examine the twig from different angles to spot any areas that need attention. Clean off any remaining pencil marks with an eraser. Stick a straight pin into the end of the twig to aid in clamping for the painting and finishing process.

TWIG: PAINTING AND FINISHING

9 ***Seal the carving.*** Make painting clamps by gluing popsicle sticks to the inside of a clothespin. Notch a dowel and glue it to the outside of the clothespin. I use 5-minute epoxy. A 2x4 with accommodating holes serves as a clamp holder. Apply three light coats of interior/exterior lacquer, letting it dry between coats. Allow the lacquer to cure for 12 hours.

10 ***Apply a coat of gesso to the twig.*** Using a stiff-bristled brush, mix a couple drops of gesso with water to the consistency of skim milk. Mix thoroughly. Prevent overlap marks by being stingy with the paint and scrubbing the entire surface of the twig. If, after drying, the twig appears evenly coated with no overlaps, one coat is enough. Clean the brush.

11 ***Apply a base coat of Payne's gray.*** Mix a small amount of Payne's gray with water to the consistency of skim milk. Evenly coat the bark areas of the twig, avoiding the ends and splits. Cover the paint in the well with a wet sponge.

12 ***Apply burnt umber.*** Mix a small amount of burnt umber with water, to the consistency of skim milk. Paint, keeping the adjacent areas clean. Stir the Payne's gray and repaint. Wash color grooves without filling in details and cover less on high areas, so highlights are automatic. When this coat is dry, re-coat with burnt umber. Repeated washes build the color evenly.

13 ***Highlight the details.*** Mix a small amount of raw sienna with water to the consistency of skim milk. Paint the exposed cambium layer on the perimeter of the ends. Use the raw sienna wash to paint the small details on the bark. Not only are the details this color, the difference in color further highlights them and makes them more noticeable. Add a couple of drops of water to the raw sienna and paint the splits and splinters on the ends. Also re-coat the cambium layer.

15 ***Enhance the darker areas.*** After the previous coat has dried, continue to retouch the darker areas with the Payne's gray. After determining how the twig will be placed in the habitat, darken the areas that will be on the bottom, enhancing the natural shading.

Tips on A Carving Work Light

I do all of my work under a 60-watt adjustable arm lamp. Keep the light low and well in front to cast a shadow from the back. This defines contours and depth as opposed to flooding the carving with light, which eliminates shadows.

14 ***Re-coat the bark.*** Stir the Payne's gray, and re-coat all of the bark. Avoid the highlighted details.

Twig habitat pattern

Photocopy at 100% or desired size.

Materials & Tools

Materials
- Tupelo, ⅜" (1cm) thick: 1" x 1½" (2.5cm x 3.8cm)
- Acrylic tube paints: raw sienna, burnt umber, Payne's gray
- Gesso
- Interior/exterior spray lacquer
- Palette (I use a plastic egg container)
- Sponges (to place over palette wells to keep paint from drying)
- Three cups of water (one each for mixing paint, initial brush cleaning, and final brush cleaning)
- Paper towels (to clean brush)
- Window cleaner with ammonia (to clean dry acrylic paint)

Tools
- Rotary tool
- Stump cutters: pear-shaped, cylinder-shaped, tapered-cylinder-shaped
- Stones: Ball-shaped, pointed
- Diamond burs: round, tapered point, pointed
- Stiff-bristled brush, camel hair brush
- Short-bristled nylon brush (to mix paint)
- Old carving knife or painting spatula (to measure paint)
- Eyedropper (to measure water to add to the acrylic paint)

Roly-Poly Hedgehog

Power carve this cute critter from a basswood egg

By Keith Dalton

These days, eggs don't just hatch birds. I've found plenty of small furry creatures hiding inside wooden eggs. With a few bits, a rotary tool, and a woodburner, you can create your own collection of egg animals.

While you can use any size wooden egg, these instructions are for a hen's egg, which is approximately 2⅜" (60mm) tall. To use a larger egg, just draw the guidelines similar to what you see in these photos.

Keith Dalton uses basswood eggs as the basis for a menagerie of carved animals.

INTERMEDIATE

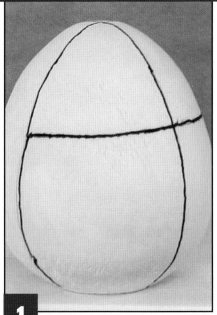

1 **Divide the egg.** Draw vertical centerlines around the egg to divide it into quarters. Then, measure down 1¼" (3.2cm) from the top of the egg and draw a horizontal line to connect three of the centerlines. This is the front.

2 **Define the top of the head.** Measure down ⅝" (1.6cm) from the top of the egg and draw a horizontal line connecting the three centerlines on the front of the egg. The second line is parallel to the horizontal line you drew in Step 1.

3 **Draw the snout.** Using the horizontal lines as top and bottom, and centering on the middle vertical line, draw a box that is ¾" (1.9cm) across the top and ⅜" (1cm) across the bottom. This box defines the hedgehog's snout.

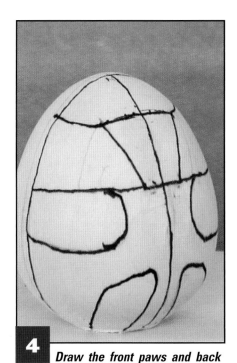

4 **Draw the front paws and back feet.** The tips of the front paws are 3⁄16" (5mm) from the vertical centerline and the paws are ⅝" (1.6cm) thick. The inside edges of the back feet are ⅛" (3mm) from the vertical centerline and the feet are ⅝" (1.6cm) thick at the top, tapering to ⅜" (1cm) at the bottom.

5 **Separate the head.** Use a ⅛" (3mm) tapered carbide-point bit to cut a ⅛" (3mm)-deep line along the horizontal line you drew in Step 1. Use the diameter of the bit to measure the depth of the cut.

6 **Define the main elements.** Use the same bit to remove the wood between the horizontal lines from the snout area back to the centerlines at the sides of the egg. Remove the wood to a depth of about 3⁄16" (5mm). Then, remove the wood around the paws to a depth of 3⁄16" (5mm).

INTERMEDIATE

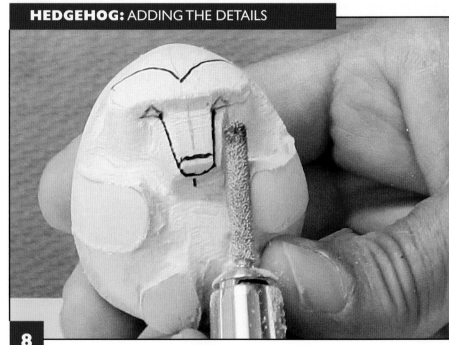

7 ***Lower the snout.*** Using a ⅛" (3mm) ball-nose, cylinder-shaped, carbide-point bit, remove wood from the entire width of the snout to a depth of ⅛" (3mm)—measure with the diameter of the bit. Only one side of the snout is lowered in the photo.

8 ***Shape the snout.*** Use the same ball-nose bit to remove wood the width of the bit on both sides of the snout, shaping and rounding the snout. Then, draw the nose, eyes, mouth, and V-shaped hairline.

9 ***Carve the face.*** Using a ³⁄₃₂" (2.5mm) pointed diamond bit, carve the eyes, nose, and mouth. Use the same bit to separate the paws from the front legs and shape the brow area, lowering the face from the area covered with spines.

10 ***Sketch in the details.*** Draw the lines between the toes, defining four toes on each paw and foot. Draw in the spines, starting at the front of the hedgehog and moving toward the back in an overlapping fish-scale pattern.

11 ***Texture the spines.*** Use a supercoarse ³⁄₃₂" (2.5mm) flame-shaped ruby bit to outline the individual spines on the hedgehog's back and legs. Work from the front of the hedgehog toward the back.

12   ***Woodburn the details.*** Outline the toes, paws, feet, and fur border with a woodburner. Then, burn the fine fur on the head and belly. Make fine, nearly parallel lines in the direction of the hair growth. Do not texture the eyes or nose.

13   ***Paint the hedgehog.*** Use black-brown acrylic paint to cover the spines. Be sure to work the paint brush down in the crevices for complete coverage. Then, paint the face, belly, and paws with a red-brown color, such as saddle brown.

14   ***Accent the face.*** Use a tan color, such as sandalwood, to dry-brush the belly, paws, and face. Paint the eyes and nose black. When dry, use a pin or toothpick to dot white highlights in the middle of each eye. Let the paint dry completely, and then spray the carving with a light coat of matte finish.

Materials & Tools

Materials:
- Basswood egg: hen size
- Pencil or fine-point marker
- Acrylic paint: red-brown, black-brown, tan, black, white
- Finish: matte spray

Tools:
- Ruler
- Rotary tool

- Kutzall carbide-point bits: ⅛" (3mm) tapered, ⅛" (3mm) ball-nose cylinder
- Diamond bit: ³⁄₃₂" (2.5mm) pointed
- Super-coarse ruby bit: ³⁄₃₂" (2.5mm) flame-shaped
- Woodburner with fine skew tip
- Paintbrushes
- Pin or toothpick

The author used these products for the project. Substitute your choice of brands, tools, and materials as desired.

Hedgehog pattern

© 2011 Woodcarving Illustrated

Carving a Cascading Ribbon Heart Pendant

Power-carved design is easy to make

By Rob Lucero

This pendant is one of my first creations, and it's still one of my favorites. I think you'll enjoy making it because it's simple and only requires a small workspace and a few easy-to-find tools. With a little patience you'll have a beautiful gift for your special someone.

I incorporated a loop in the pendant design because I broke quite a few pendants trying to drill a hole in the top after they were finished. If it didn't break during the drilling process, it would sometimes break while gluing the silver loop in. Gluing can be a very messy process. The new design is much cleaner and produces fewer broken pendants, as well as a happier woodworker.

If you have any questions about making this pendant, you're welcome to e-mail me through my website or Facebook. I'm happy to share any tips I have.

Heart pendant patterns

© 2012 Woodcarving Illustrated

PENDANT: PREPARING THE BLANK

1 ***Prepare the blank.*** Trace the pattern onto the blank. Mark the waste areas with an X. Use a scroll saw or a band saw to cut the outline of the pendant. Then, go back and cut the details. Drill a ³⁄₆₄" (1.5mm)-diameter hole through the blank for the loop.

2 ***Refine the pattern on the blank.*** Using a ruler and pencil, and using the pattern as a guide, draw straight lines from the inner corners of the cut portions to the bottom of the outer edge on the front and back of the pendant. Mark the shaded areas that will be carved away.

3 ***Begin carving the pendant.*** Carve away about ¹⁄₁₆" (2mm) of wood from the shaded areas on the front and back of the pendant. I use a ¹⁄₁₆" (2mm)-diameter ball-shaped engraving bit. Work slowly to keep from nicking the sides. The goal is to keep the surface as smooth as possible.

4 ***Smooth the carved areas.*** Use a flat needle file to smooth the recessed areas of the pendant. When you're finished, you should have raised flat surfaces and recessed flat surfaces. It is easy to break the pendant when using the files. Support the back of the piece and use light pressure on the file.

5 ***Refine the pendant.*** Round the edges of the raised surfaces with a flat needle file. Smooth the edges of the recessed areas with the flat edge of a half-round file.

6 ***Sand the pendant.*** Use a small piece of fine-grit sandpaper to smooth the surface of the pendant. A well-sanded surface will help ensure a smooth finish.

PENDANT: FINISHING THE PROJECT

7 ***Apply the finish.*** Spray high-gloss finish on the front and sides of the pendant. Allow the finish to dry, turn the pendant over, and apply the finish to the back. I apply three to four coats of finish to the piece, allowing the finish to dry between coats.

Materials & Tools

Materials:
- Poplar, ¼" (6mm) thick: 2" x 3" (5.1cm x 7.6cm)
- Sandpaper: fine grit
- Finish: high gloss spray

Tools:
- Scroll saw and blades: #12

- Rotary-power carver with bits: ¹⁄₁₆" (2mm)-diameter ball-shaped high-speed steel engraving bit
- Needle files: half-round, flat
- Drill with bit: ³⁄₆₄" (1.5mm) diameter

The author used these products for the project.
Substitute your choice of brands, tools, and materials as desired.

Carving a Rattle Stick

Combine wood spirits with a ball-in-cage to create a unique walking stick

By Steve Buchholz
Step-by-step photos by
Michelle Buchholz

I have been carving for years, and I used to spend a lot of time in the woods looking for sticks. But once word got out that I carve, I worked out a deal with people that if they gave me three sticks, I'd carve one for them.

I often make these ball-in-cage rattle sticks to fulfill the deal. If you are walking in the woods, especially during berry- or mushroom-gathering season, you can easily startle a bear, which is a very bad thing. If your stick rattles with every step, there's no way to surprise a bear. My wife and I carry rattle sticks any time we're in the woods.

Like most carvings in found wood, the stick determines the overall shape and design of the project. With this stick, the cage at the top ended up a bit too fragile to be completely functional. But with a few design changes or a slightly different branch, you can have a functional, durable, and beautiful carved stick.

Choosing the Sticks

I look for branches on downed trees that are 2" to 3" (5.1cm to 7.6cm) thick with long straight sections. I use red fir or larch wood, which are common in my area, but you can use nearly any wood; the harder and denser the wood, the more detail you can carve into it.

RATTLE STICK: PREPARING THE STICK

1 ***Remove the bark.*** Remove any loose bark by hand, and then use an old knife or drawknife to remove as much bark as you can without carving into the stick. Preserve any sap lines or other interesting natural characteristics as much as possible. On some sticks, I remove bark only from the area I plan to carve; on other sticks, I remove all of the bark.

2 ***Refine the stick.*** Use a 60-grit sanding drum in a rotary-power carver to remove the tough inner bark. Then, use the same bit to remove any unwanted limb ends and any soft or decayed wood. Make sure the area you plan to carve is sanded smooth.

3 ***Carve the top of the cage.*** Use the 60-grit sanding drum to round and shape the top of the stick. With most sticks, one or two areas will be denser than the rest of the stick. Determine the dense areas as you carve the top and plan to position the faces in these dense areas.

RATTLE STICK: CARVING THE CAGE

4 ***Rough out the cage.*** Use the same sanding drum to rough out the shape of the cage. You can use the pattern as a guide, but I often just freehand carve the cage using my imagination or any natural features on the wood. Remember, the bottom of the cage will become the forehead of the wood spirit. For this carving, I bring the cage farther down on the back to act as hair for the forehead of the second wood spirit.

5 ***Define the cage bars.*** I use a long, tapered, carbide-point bit to carve out the wood around the ball. Keep the cage bars as thick as possible. The thicker the bars, the more durable the carving will be. Don't remove too much wood from inside the cage. You need to carve a large enough ball that it will rattle.

6 ***Free the ball.*** I use a spiral cutter, such as a ⁵⁄₃₂" (4mm)-diameter Rotozip bit. Carefully cut inside the woven bars to carve the top of the ball. Remove the excess wood above the ball and create a curved opening at the top of the cage. Then, remove the excess wood from under the ball. Switch to a ⅛" (3mm) spiral cutter to free the sides of the ball.

7 ***Refine the cage.*** Hand-sand the inside and outside of the cage with 120-grit sandpaper to remove the tool marks. Repeat the process with 220-grit sandpaper. Don't worry about making the cage perfectly smooth. Use a triangular high-speed steel cutter and a light touch to carve hair texture into the cage bars. If you use a slightly dull bit, it will burn the wood slightly and give you more texture. Hand-sand the cage again with 220-grit sandpaper.

8 ***Refine the forehead and cage.*** Use the triangular high-speed steel cutter to undercut the areas where one bar weaves under another. Then, use the same bit to undercut the bars/hairline above the forehead. I carve a face on both sides of the stick, with the face on the opposite side staggered underneath the first face. **Note:** For this and subsequent steps, complete the process on the higher face, and then repeat the process on the lower face.

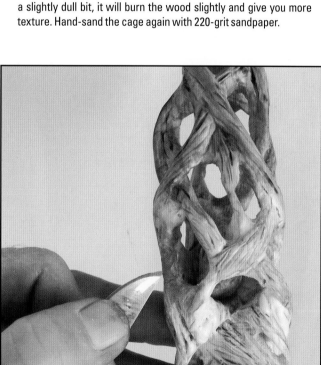

9 ***Seal the cage.*** Stain the cage with golden pecan stain. When the stain is dry, apply a coat of clear satin polyurethane to seal the wood. If you don't finish and seal the cage fast enough, the changes in moisture in the stick may cause the wood to crack or split. To fix a broken cage bar, glue the wood back together with stainable foaming glue and use wood putty to fill any gaps. Use a knife to carve the putty to match the rest of the bar. Use a triangular high-speed steel cutter to texture the putty, and then sand it with 600-grit sandpaper.

RATTLE STICK: CARVING THE FACES

10 ***Rough out the nose and eyes.*** Use the tapered carbide-point bit to deepen the hairline and carve away the wood around the eyebrows. Carve out the eye sockets under the brows and along the nose line. Shape the nose, leaving plenty of wood for the mustache. Separate the cheeks using light strokes from the eye sockets down along the nose line.

11 ***Carve the cheeks and mustache.*** Use the triangular high-speed steel cutter to carve in from the bottom of the nose down along the top of the mustache. Use light downward strokes until you've given the cheekbones good definition. Wrap the mustache around the stick to become a part of the cage hairline for the lower face.

12 ***Carve the mouth.*** Draw the mouth below the mustache. Use the long tapered carbide-point bit to carve out the mouth between the mustache and lower lip. Use light upward strokes. Shape the bottom lip and separate the mustache from the lips and face. Add texture to the mustache.

13 ***Rough in the beard.*** Use the sanding drum to carve the rough beard texture. The beard should flow in long locks. Use light strokes to weave the beard around the stick to join the mustache and beard of the lower face, creating one large beard for both faces.

14 ***Refine the beard and mustache.*** Use the tapered carbide-point bit to carve the weaving locks of the beard. The locks in the beard echo the weaving bars of the cage. Continue refining the beard around the side of the stick to join with the beard of the other face.

15 ***Refine the eyes.*** Use the triangular high-speed steel cutter to deepen the eye sockets. Use a sanding drum to remove wood under the eyes to create bags. Then, use the sanding drum to shape the eyelids. Use a small tapered diamond bit to add more depth.

16 ***Finish carving the eyes.*** Use the small tapered diamond bit to carve the top and bottom eyelids. I create open eyes on the higher face and closed eyes on the lower face. On the lower face, just carve the slight separation and make sure the top eyelid goes over the bottom eyelid. On the higher face, carve visible eyeballs between the lids and deep holes to represent the pupils.

Experiment with different faces or add a carved chain on the top of the stick.

Hand-sand the stick to remove all of the tool marks and smooth the beard. Then, apply golden pecan stain to the carving. After the stain is dry, apply clear satin spray polyurethane finish. Buff between coats of polyurethane with 0000 steel wool. Apply as many coats of finish as it takes to give the stick a soft feel and appearance.

Materials & Tools

Materials:
- Branch: 3" (7.6cm) diameter and as long as possible
- Stain, such as Minwax Golden Pecan
- Polyurethane: spray satin
- Sandpaper: assorted up to 600-grit
- Steel wool: 0000

The author used these products for the project. Substitute your choice of brands, tools, and materials as desired.

Tools:
- Chainsaw or hand saw (to harvest stick)
- Drawknife or pocketknife
- Rotary-power carver and bits: sanding drum with 60-grit drum; long, tapered, carbide-point bit; small diamond carving bit; triangular high-speed steel cutter; spiral cutters, such as 5/32" (4mm)- and 1/8" (3mm)-diameter
- Rotozip cutters

Rattle stick patterns

Patterns below are drawn to scale on a 1" grid. Enlarge or reduce to desired size.

© 2012 Woodcarving Illustrated

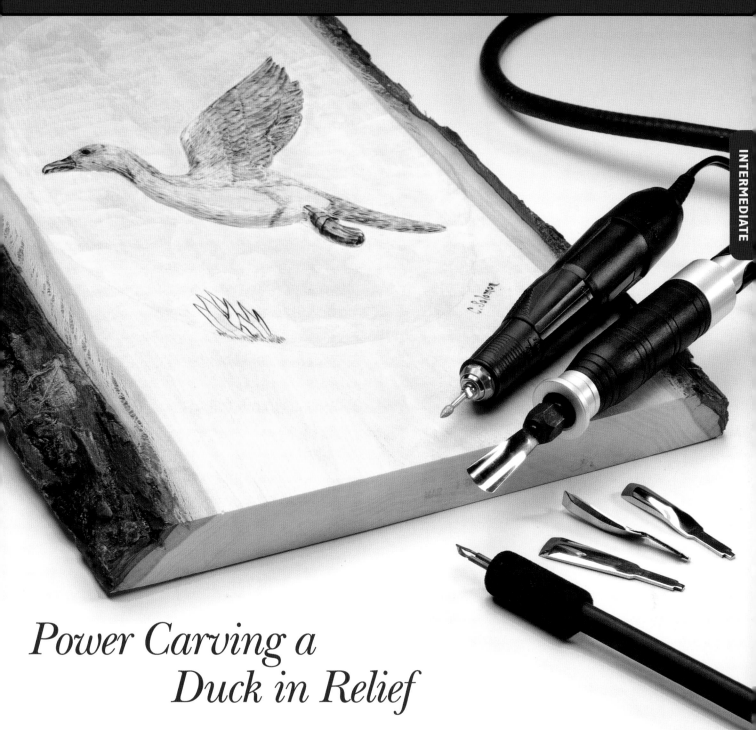

INTERMEDIATE

Power Carving a Duck in Relief

Simple pintail duck is a great introduction to reciprocating tools

By Chuck Solomon and Dave Hamilton

This basic relief project combines techniques for using reciprocating tools, traditional-edge tools, rotary bits, and a woodburner. If you don't have a reciprocating handpiece, use a piece of scrap wood to practice lowering the background with aggressive carbide-point bits in a rotary power carver.

The northern pintail duck can be found throughout North America and northern areas of Europe and Asia. We have both had the opportunity to view and study pintail ducks at

numerous national wildlife refuges and other wetland areas. It is a thrill to see hundreds of pintails rise off of the water early in the morning.

We chose a slab of basswood with bark remaining on the sides to provide a natural frame. Use graphite paper to transfer the pattern to the blank and sketch an oval around the design. Leave at least ¼" (6mm) between the oval and any part of the duck.

INTERMEDIATE

1 *Outline the pattern.* Carve a stop cut along the perimeter of the pattern with a ¼" (6mm)-wide V-tool in a reciprocating carver. Cut approximately ⅛" (3mm) outside of the pattern line.

2 *Lower the background.* Use a ¾" (19mm)-wide fishtail gouge in a reciprocating carver to lower the area between the oval and the pattern. Remove the wood in several passes. Reposition the blank as needed to make the smoothest cuts. Slope the wood from the oval to the cuts next to the duck.

3 *Clean up the gouge marks.* Go back over the background with the same fishtail gouge to clean up and smooth the surface. Switch to a handheld ¾" (19mm)-wide fishtail gouge to provide more control, especially near the duck.

4 *Separate the wings.* Carve along the line separating the wings with a V-tool in the reciprocating carver. Use a fishtail gouge to lower the back wing slightly, creating the effect of the back wing being behind the front wing.

5 *Round the duck's body.* Round the body with a pear-shaped stump cutter in the flexible shaft tool. Use a high speed (14,000 rpm or greater) for best control. Clean up the edges by hand sanding with 250-grit Swiss sanding cloth. Do not round the wing tips.

6 *Outline the wing feathers.* Remove the wood between the tips of the feathers with a bench knife or a safe-end cylinder-shaped diamond bit and a flame-shaped ruby or diamond bit. Make a shallow stop cut alongside each wing feather with a bench knife. Carve between each feather with a safe-end cylinder-shaped diamond bit.

7 **_Carve the back wing._** Sketch in the feathers on the back wing. The front wing shows the underside of the wing and full top primary feathers. On the back wing, we are viewing the top of the wing and only see part of the top primary feathers. Stop cut along each feather with a bench knife and carve between the feathers with a safe-end cylinder-shaped diamond bit.

8 **_Carve a depression in the front wing._** Use a ½" (13mm)-diameter ball-shaped stump cutter to carve a shallow depression in the front wing. The ¼" (6mm)-deep depression, located in front of the covert feathers, should be less than 1" (35mm) wide.

9 **_Burn the flight feathers._** Wood-burn the primary, secondary, tertial, and covert feathers on the wings. Use a ⅜" (10mm)-wide skew-tip woodburning pen. Keep the burn lines curved at the top and keep them as close together as possible.

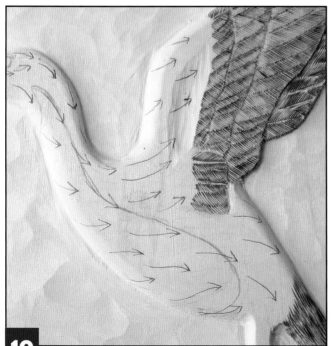

10 **_Sketch the body feathers._** Outline the location of the back tail feathers, rump, white body feathers of the lower breast and body, the brown feathers on the head and neck, and the dark feathers on the back and sides. Sketch in the direction of the feather flow.

11 **_Woodburn the body feathers._** Use a higher temperature to burn the black tail feathers and rump. Keep these lines close to each other. The darker body feathers are burned at a lower temperature and are farther apart. The white feather areas are burned at an even lower temperature and the lines are even farther apart.

12

Woodburn the bill, eye, and foot.
Use a ⅛" (3mm)-wide shader burning pen
for the bill and the foot. Outline and burn
the eye with a writing tip burning pen.

13

Clean up the woodburned areas.
Use a soft rotary brush in the flexible shaft
tool at a low speed (less than 5,000 rpm)
to remove any residue left from the woodburning pens. Brush in the direction of the
burning. Strengthen the feather tips and
any other areas that could break with thin
cyanoacrylate (CA) glue.

14

Add the grass. Sketch the clump
of wetland grass or other vegetation on a
copy of the pattern and then transfer the
design to the blank. Use a skew woodburning pen to burn in the grass.

15

Apply the finish. Apply a light coat of Deft spray satin finish. Let it dry for 15 to 45 minutes. Go over the duck with a soft
rotary brush at a low speed (less than 5,000 rpm). Apply one to
two additional coats of Deft, allowing it to dry between coats.
Use a soft rotary brush on the duck between coats and after you
apply the final coat. Attach a hanger to the back of the carving.

Materials & Tools

Materials:
- Basswood, 1" (2.5cm) thick: 10" x 14" (25.4cm x 35.6cm)
- Sanding cloth, Swiss: 250 grit
- Cyanoacrylate (CA) glue, thin
- Finish: spray satin, such as Deft

Tools:
- Flexible shaft machine with a standard handpiece
- Reciprocating carver or handpiece
- Reciprocating gouges: ¾" (19mm) fishtail gouge;
  ¼" (6mm)-wide V-tool
- Ball-shaped stump cutter: ¼" (6mm) dia.
- Pear-shaped stump cutter: ¼" (6mm) dia.
- Safe-end cylinder-shaped diamond bit
- Flame-shaped ruby or diamond bit
- Soft rotary bristle brush
- Woodburner with tips: ⅜" (10mm)-wide skew,
  ⅜" (10mm)-wide shader, writing tip
- Fishtail palm gouge: ¾" (19mm)
- Carving knife

Duck relief pattern

© 2010 Woodcarving Illustrated

Making a Realistic Bluegill Pin

Use power carving tools and an airbrush to create a realistic fish pin

By Dave Arndt

At various carving shows over the years, I have noticed several carvers making songbird and duck pins. As a decorative fish carver, I thought a fish pin would be a nice addition to my table display. I chose the bluegill for this article because it's a popular species. Many of the carving and painting steps can be adapted to a different species once you have a pattern. You can turn your bluegill into a refrigerator magnet simply by replacing the pin with a small magnet.

Before you begin carving, gather some reference photos of bluegills. Good quality photos can be found in fishing magazines, and they really help you get the details right.

Because this project is small, a high-quality detail airbrush makes the painting easier. It's possible to use a brush with wet-on-wet blending techniques, but practice on scrap wood before trying to paint your project. Refer to your reference photos often, and apply the color a little at a time. I mix several paint colors with equal parts of basecoat/sealer to keep from applying too much pigment, which can lead to a dark paint job.

Cutting the Blank

Start by cutting the blank. Cover one side of the blank with clear packaging tape, which lubricates the scroll saw blade during cutting and makes the pattern easy to remove after cutting. Apply spray adhesive to the taped side of the blank and the back of the pattern. Turn the pattern face up and press it onto the blank. Use a scroll saw to cut the profile of the bluegill. Do not remove the pattern yet. Position the pin on the back of the blank and mark the location with a pencil. Use a knife to make stop cuts along the lines, and then use a ¼" (6mm)-wide bent chisel to carve a shallow mortise for the pin.

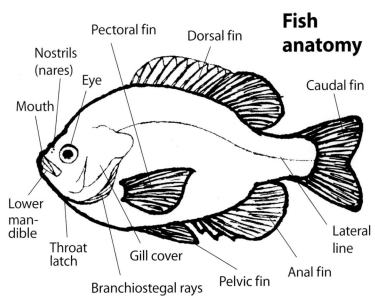

Fish anatomy

Nostrils (nares)

Pectoral fin

Dorsal fin

Eye

Caudal fin

Mouth

Lower man-dible

Throat latch

Gill cover

Branchiostegal rays

Pelvic fin

Anal fin

Lateral line

1 ***Burn the body lines.*** Use a woodburner with a small skew tip to burn through the paper and tape along the lines that separate the dorsal, anal, pectoral, and pelvic fins from the body. Then, burn the rear of the gill flap to define the head. Peel the tape off the wood to remove the pattern from the blank.

2 ***Define the fins.*** Use a ¼" (6mm)-diameter safe-end tapered-cylinder carbide-point bit to rough out the dorsal and anal fins. Switch to a safe-end tapered cylinder diamond bit to refine the fins until they are about ³⁄₃₂" (2.5mm) from the body. Then, remove some wood from the rear of the gill flap following the burned line down to the throat latch. Define the pectoral fin along the burned line using the same technique, refining the belly area and pelvic fin as you shape.

3 ***Shape the tail.*** Use the pattern as a guide as you define the tail (caudal fin) and separate it from the body. Use a round-end tapered cylinder diamond bit. Give the tail some movement by removing wood from the back to create a bend. Shape the tail until its thickness matches that of the other fins. Use a ⁵⁄₃₂" (4mm)-diameter ball-shaped diamond bit to remove wood from the center of the pectoral fin to give it a concave shape.

4 ***Add the details to the head.*** Use a bit of your choice to round the head. Use a pencil or graphite paper to transfer the pattern lines to the head, and then burn them. Use a small safe-end cylinder-shaped diamond bit to remove wood below and behind the lines to make the features stand out. Use the same bit to continue shaping the head using the pattern and project photos as guides.

5 ***Locate the eye.*** Transfer the eye location onto the blank. Use a ⅛" (3mm)-diameter ball-shaped diamond bit to carve a socket that will accept a #61 ball-head straight pin. Adjust the depth of the socket until the ball is recessed at least half-way into the head. Remove the pin and use its pointed end to create the nostrils (nares). Lightly burn the boney plates under the chin that connect to the gills (the branchiostegal rays). Lightly sand the body with 220-grit sandpaper.

BLUEGILL: REFINING THE FISH

6 ***Add the fin details.*** Use a pencil to draw the fin spines and rays. Use a ¹⁄₃₂" (1mm)-diameter ball-shaped diamond bit to remove wood between the spines of the dorsal and anal fins, and between the rays on the soft fins (the tail and the soft dorsal, pectoral, and pelvic fins). Use a small pointed diamond bit laid on its side to shape the fin spines. Don't make the spines too thin or pointed, or they will break off. Use the wood burning pen to create the fin rays on the soft fins.

7 ***Create the lateral line.*** Draw the lateral line with a pencil. Flatten a nail or piece of wire and lightly press this shop-made tool along the line. Sand the surface of the surrounding wood until it is level with the bottom of the pressed line. Paint clean water along the pressed-down line with a small artist brush. As the wood dries, the lateral line will rise above the surrounding wood. Practice on a scrap of wood to learn how much pressure to use when pressing in the line.

8 ***Add the scales to the body.*** Sketch intersecting diagonal lines across the body and on the cheek area of the head. Use a very small stylus to trace over the pencil marks, gently pressing them into the wood. Use an eraser to remove the pencil lines, and then seal the wood with Minwax Wood Hardener to strengthen the fins without making them brittle. Allow the sealer to dry overnight.

BLUEGILL: PAINTING THE FISH

9 ***Prime the fish.*** Use removable adhesive putty to attach a craft stick to the back of the carving to serve as a handle during the painting process. Apply a few coats of white primer or gesso and allow it to dry. Use blue painter's tape to mask off all of the fins. Apply the torn edge of the masking tape next to the body to eliminate any sharp edges in the paint lines. Use a hobby knife to trim the tape around the pectoral fin.

10 ***Paint the base color.*** Spray Createx silver below the lateral line and on the lower gill cover. Spray Createx gold above the lateral line, fading it into the silver just below the lateral line and on the upper part of the gill cover. Apply 401 satin white pearl on the lower side of the front of the anal fin and under the lower mandible. Add a few drops of 90 bright orange to some 140 cadmium yellow and apply a light coat of the mixture to the lower cheeks, throat, and lower side. Remove the masking tape from the anal fin and apply a light coat of the same mixture to the anal fin.

11 ***Darken the belly.*** Mask off the head and the branchiostegal rays from the body. Spray the throat area with 90 bright orange, fading out at the rear of the pectoral fin. Remove the masking tape from the head and use 10 white and a small artist brush to paint the branchiostegal rays. Then, apply a second coat to the branchiostegal rays with 401 satin white pearl.

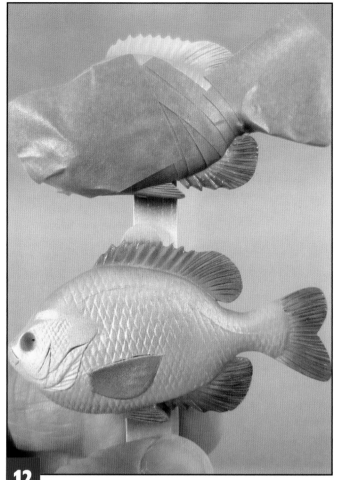

12 ***Paint the fins.*** Remove the masking tape from the dorsal fins, and apply 61 medium bass green lightly to the top of the head, back, tail, and dorsal fins. Then, apply 340 transpar brown to the same areas. Remove the masking tape from the pelvic fin. Mask off the body around the pelvic and anal fins. Mix equal parts 672 candy, Payne's gray and 100 basecoat, and spray the mixture onto the pelvic and anal fins. Unmask the body and spray the mixture on the tail and dorsal fins. Mix equal parts 10 white and 100 basecoat, and lightly spray the dorsal fins, anal fin, and tail.

13 ***Color the body.*** Mix equal parts 320 transpar violet and 100 basecoat, and lightly spray the mixture along the side of the body above the pectoral fin and below the lateral line. The color should fade away half way to the tail. Then, unmask the pectoral fin and mask off the body around it.

14 ***Paint the pectoral fin and gill.*** Add a few drops of 90 bright orange to 140 cadmium yellow and spray the pectoral fin. Spray the pectoral fin with 90 bright orange, and then 340 transpar brown. Mix equal parts of 672 candy Payne's gray and 100 basecoat. Add a few drops of 300 sailfish blue to 10 white, and thin the mixture with water. Use an artist's brush to apply the mixture to the lower edge of the gill cover, using your reference photos as a guide.

BLUEGILL: PAINTING THE DETAILS

15 ***Add the bar pattern.*** Mix equal parts 64 detail green with 100 basecoat. Dip a 3/0 artist's brush in the paint, blot it on a paper towel, and then apply the mixture to the fish. Use the reference photos as guides to create the broken-line bar pattern. Use this mixture in the airbrush to lightly spray the top of the head and back to darken these areas slightly.

16 ***Paint the gill flap.*** Mask off the body around the gill flap and spray the gill flap with 65 detail black. Use the same color to spray the dark spot on the soft dorsal fin. Unmask the body and paint the entire fish with a coat of 360 gold toner.

17 ***Apply iridescent powders.*** Use a small flat brush to apply 442 gold power to the back above the lateral line and to the scaled area on the gill cover. Keep the powder off the fins. Apply a coat of 100 basecoat over the powders to lock them in place. Brush on 441 green powder along the lateral line and lock it in place with a shot of 100 basecoat. Use the same technique to apply 444 violet powder along the side above the pectoral fin and above the lateral line.

18 ***Add the eye.*** Press the ball head pin into a piece of scrap wood and apply a coat of 65 detail black followed by a coat of Createx gold. Then, apply a coat of 71 burnt umber followed by a coat of 61 medium bass green. Allow the paint to dry thoroughly, and then use a pair of diagonal pliers to cut the pin just below the ball. Add a drop of cyanoacrylate (CA) glue to the eye socket and press the eye into place. Use a magnifier, a steady hand, and a small artist's brush to add a pupil with 65 detail black.

19 ***Finish the pin.*** Apply two coats of Krylon clear gloss finish and allow it to dry. Then, use two-part five-minute epoxy to attach the pin to the mortise on the back.

Bluegill pin patterns

© 2013 Woodcarving Illustrated

Materials & Tools

Materials:
- Tupelo or basswood, 5⁄16" (8mm) thick with flat-sawn grain: 1⅝" x 2¾" (4.1cm x 7cm)
- Tape: clear packaging; blue painter's
- Spray adhesive
- Pencil
- Ball-head pin: #61
- Sandpaper: 220 grit
- Wood hardener, such as Minwax
- Removable adhesive putty
- Craft stick
- Primer, such as Krylon: white
- Airbrush paints: Createx brand—gold, silver; Polytranspar water-based—401 satin white pearl, 90 bright orange, 140 cadmium yellow, 10 white, 61 medium bass green, 340 transpar brown, 320 transpar purple, 300 sailfish blue, 64 detail green, 65 detail black, 360 gold toner, 71 burnt umber; Lifetone Hydromist—100 basecoat/sealer, 672 candy Payne's gray
- Iridescent powders, such as Polytranspar: 441 shimmering green, 442 shimmering gold, 444 shimmering violet
- Cyanoacrylate (CA) glue
- 5-minute epoxy

- Clear finish, such as Krylon: gloss
- Pin back

Tools:
- Scroll saw and blades
- Bent chisel: ¼" (6mm) wide
- Woodburner with small skew tip
- Micro motor or flexible shaft machine with bits: ¼" (6mm)-diameter safe-end tapered-cylinder shaped carbide-point, small safe-end cylinder-shaped diamond, small tapered cone diamond, small tapered diamond, 1⁄32" (1mm)-diameter ball-shaped diamond, ⅛" (3mm)-diameter ball-shaped diamond, 5⁄32" (4mm)-diameter ball-shaped diamond
- Paintbrushes: 3/0 round, 12/0 round, #4 shader
- Small stylus
- Flattened nail or piece of wire
- Detail airbrush, such as a Badger Velocity
- Hobby knife
- Diagonal pliers

The author used these products for the project. Substitute your choice of brands, tools, and materials as desired.

The American Woodcock

By Frank Russell

The woodcock project was presented as a 1998 seminar at my Stonegate Woodcarving School, and the photographs and carving sequences shown were taken as I taught.

The woodcock can be posed on a base in a strutting position, in a legs-down position, or without legs showing with chest and wing edges nestled on a base of leaves or forest litter. I often find them in this position when I wander through alder swamps and thickets. The position I used for this project also suggests a nesting bird.

As with any carving project, surround yourself with definitive and detailed references. You can't carve what you don't know. Generally, your carving is only as good as your best reference.

Materials & Tools

Materials:
- Tupelo, 4" (10.2cm) thick: 5" x 9" (12.7cm x 22.9cm)
- Poster board
- Glue stick
- Hobby knife or scissors
- Glass eye (optional)
- Finishing materials

Tools:
- Bandsaw or scroll saw
- 4 TPI skip-tooth blade
- Rotary tool with bits (see chart page 142)

1 ***Make patterns.*** Using the working drawings, enlarge the side and top views and glue them to a piece of poster board with a glue stick. Cut the outlines out with a hobby knife or scissors. The woodcock can also be carved in a different scale: one-third, half, or quarter scale, for example.

2 ***Cut the block.*** Use the top and bottom waste pieces to cradle the blank. Tape the three pieces together with masking tape before cutting the top view.

3 ***Mark the blank.*** Draw a centerline around the entire bird. Carve the bird with the head straight. Draw the top of the head, the beak, a shoulder line, and the upper line of the dropped wing. Use a broken line for the belly position. Leave plenty of stock for the wing curvature.

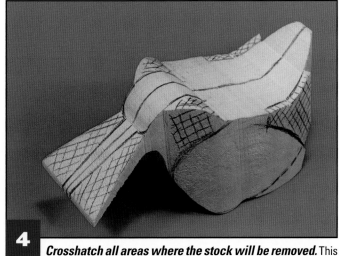

4 ***Crosshatch all areas where the stock will be removed.*** This is a safety reminder that allows you to more easily observe the symmetry of the entire bird. Crosshatching also reminds you to go back to areas that should be reshaped or don't look right.

5 ***Using a flame-shaped carbide bit (1), remove all crosshatched areas.*** Be sure to maintain symmetry from side to side. Carefully remove wood along both sides of the beak, and don't allow the bit to run around the front tip. Keep everything square at this point.

6 ***Remove the waste wood between the legs.*** Use the same flame-shaped bit to remove the crosshatched area between the legs on the underside of the bird.

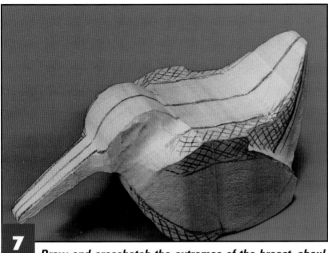

7 *Draw and crosshatch the extremes of the breast, shoulders, and sides of the tail.*

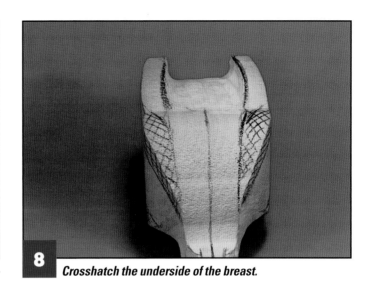

8 *Crosshatch the underside of the breast.*

9 ***Remove wood.*** With bit #1 or #2, remove crosshatched areas, rounding toward the centerline.

WOODCOCK: SHAPING THE BODY

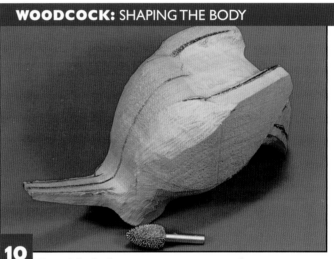

10 ***Round the body.*** As you round the body, think of the egg that this bird came from. Don't leave semi-rounded corners.

11 ***Draw the head, bill, and major body areas.*** Using a pencil, draw the extremes of the head and bill and crosshatch the areas to be removed. Draw shapes of major body contours and feather depressions such as the nape, cape, tail coverts, and wings.

12 ***Draw the bib and breast.***

13 ***Shape the major contours.*** Use the small, flame-shaped carbide bit (#4) and a large, flame-shaped ruby carver (#5). Make the contours gracefully rounded and shaped to indicate which feather groups lie on top of one another.

15 ***Contour the areas in the previous step.*** Use bits #4 and #5. Again, make all contours gracefully rounded and shaped to indicate which groups lie on top or under one another.

17 ***Draw the tail feathers, tail coverts, and back feathers in preparation for rough shaping.*** Also draw the hard wing feathers such as the primaries, secondaries, and tertials.

14 ***Draw the feather groups.*** Draw the individual feathers on the tail. Indicate the extremes of wing covert groups, tertials, and secondaries.

16 ***Draw the body feathers on the underside of the bird.*** This prepares for the rough shaping of the softer-appearing under feathers.

18 ***Outline the feathers.*** Do the tail feathers, tertials, lower wing coverts, secondaries, and primaries with the bent, skew-tipped woodburner (#12). Outline and shape the contour feathers (tail coverts, back, upper wing coverts, cape, and nape) with the large and small flame-shaped ruby carvers (#5 and #6). Finish shape and smooth with the tapered steel bur (#8).

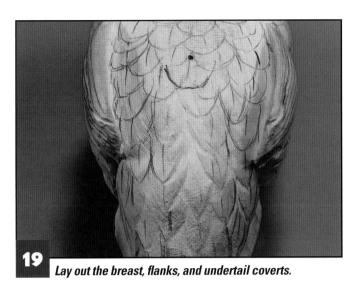

19 *Lay out the breast, flanks, and undertail coverts.*

20 *Finish shape the breast, flank, and undertail coverts.* Use bits #6 and #8. Relieve and outline the bottoms of the tail feathers. Make sure that the upper side of each tail feather corresponds with its underside. What is seen on the bottom must correspond with what is on the top.

WOODCOCK: CARVING THE BILL

21 *Rough shape the bill and draw the eyes.* Make the bill square. Then, draw the locations of eyes. At this time, draw the extremes of the jowl-ear area.

22 *Lay out the details of the bill.* Crosshatch the areas where you need the most control when removing wood. Also, lay out the underside of the bill.

23 *Finish shape and smooth all areas of the bill.* Use bits #6 and #8. Use 220-grit sandpaper to smooth the wood. Use the same bits to finish shape and smooth the underside of the bill.

24 *Cut in the bill separation and nostrils with the skew-tipped woodburner (#13).* Begin with a low heat setting until you establish the desired line. Then, increase the heat to deepen it. Cut in each eye cavity using the ball-shaped ruby carver (#7). Lay out and shape all head feathers.

INTERMEDIATE

25 **Set the eyes.** Use 10mm brown for a full-size woodcock. Be sure to texture the feathered areas around the eyes before placing. A texturing stone can ruin the glass. If the eyes are set before texturing is finished, cover the eye with a circular piece of electrician's tape.

27 **Final shape and smooth the feathers.** Do this over the entire bird in preparation for texturing.

26 *Lay out any remaining feather areas that were not done.*

WOODCOCK: TEXTURING

28 **Pre-texture all major feather groups with a ball-shaped bit** *(#9).* Keep the strokes in the same direction that you want the barbules of the feather to go. This makes the finish texturing much easier and gives the finished feather the little "bumps and rolls" that a real feather has.

Feather Texturing

I texture all working or stiff feathers with a woodburner. I find that burning in texture gives these feathers the same hard or stiff look that actual feathers have.

I texture all feathers that I consider contour or soft feathers with a cylinder-shaped or inverted cone texturing stone (#10 and #11). The stone gives these feathers a softer look than burning does.

I pre-texture all feathers, except the tiny ones on the head, with a ball-shaped stone (#9). The size of the feather determines the size of the ball shape I use. On a bird such as the woodcock, I can accomplish the entire pre-texturing operation with just one size.

29 *Texture all the stiffer-appearing working feathers with the skewed-tipped woodburner (#13).* There may be areas where you are unable to get the feathered effect that you want with a wood burner. You can achieve a rougher looking feather edge by selectively texturing over the burn-textured edge with a cylinder-shaped or inverted cone texturing stone (#10 and #11).

30 *Finish texture the remaining bird with the cylinder-shaped or inverted cone texturing stone (#10 and #11).* Take the carving outdoors and check it under bright sunlight. More often than not, you will find one or more sections that could stand a bit of touchup with a texturing bit or wood burner. Then, the woodcock is ready for sealing, gessoing, and painting.

Legs and Feet

This project was designed to pose the finished bird in one of four positions:

1. Standing erect in a strutting pose with fully exposed legs and feet. This is a common position in the spring during mating season with the legs side by side or with the legs in a striding or walking position.

2. Standing in a crouched position with partially exposed legs and feet. The woodcock often stands in this position while listening for worm and grub movement underground.

3. Resting on the ground with no legs or feet showing. The toes may be partially exposed depending on depth of ground cover.

4. Nesting with body sunk deeply into ground cover. Showing toes is optional.

Unless well reinforced with wire, I do not think that commercially cast woodcock feet will support a bird of this size without bending or breaking. If carving for competition, I find most sponsoring organizations frown on cast feet anyway.

I prefer to make the feet and legs of a wildfowl myself. I can position my carving in any manner I want without fear of the legs breaking or the loss of the bird's natural appearance.

I do buy commercially cast bird feet for reference and sizing when I don't have a good natural specimen to work from. Along with the cast feet, I use photos of live specimens. Many consider using cast feet as a cheat, but used or not, they are invaluable as a reference. If the bird is not a competition bird, and it is in the resting position, I do use parts of the cast feet. I simply cut the toes off, sharpen the details with a jeweler's file if necessary, paint them, and use them under the bird.

No matter what the method of construction, realism is imperative so that the feet don't detract from the fine detail of the carving. When I am judging, I often see a good wildfowl carving that has poorly constructed feet. No matter what the quality of the carving, it doesn't place or, at best, it receives a lesser award.

Carving Bits and Texturing Tools Schedule

INTERMEDIATE

Bit/Tool Number	Head Shape	Description	Head Size	Shaft Diameter
1	Flame	Carbide bit	¾" dia. x 1" long (19mm x 25mm)	¼" (6mm)
2	Cylinder	Carbide bit	¾" dia. x ⅞" long (19mm x 22mm)	¼" (6mm)
3	Flame	Carbide bit	⅜" dia. x ½" long (10mm x 13mm)	⅛" (3mm)
4	Flame	Carbide bit	¼" dia. x ⅜" long (6mm x 10mm)	$3/32$" (2.5mm)
5	Flame	Ruby carver	¼" dia. x ⅜" long (6mm x 10mm)	$3/32$" (2.5mm)
6	Flame	Ruby carver	⅛" dia. x ¼" long (3mm x 6mm)	$3/32$" (2.5mm)
7	Ball	Ruby carver	⅛" (3mm) dia.	$3/32$" (2.5mm)
8	Tapered	Steel-fluted bur	⅛" dia. x 1/4" long (3mm x 6mm)	$3/32$" (2.5mm)
9	Ball	Aluminum/chrome oxide	⅛" (3mm) dia.	$3/32$" (2.5mm)
10	Cylinder	Aluminum/chrome oxide	$3/32$" dia. x ¼" long (2.5mm x 6mm)	$3/32$" (2.5mm)
11	Inverted Cone	Aluminum/chrome oxide	⅛" (3mm) dia.	$3/32$" (2.5mm)
12	Bent Skew (dull edge)	Woodburner	$5/16$" (8mm) wide	N/A
13	Skew (straight edge)	Woodburner	⅜" (10mm) wide	N/A

American Woodcock patterns

INTERMEDIATE

Photocopy at 100%

Beak Cross Section

10mm Eye (Full Scale)

Side View

Lower Tail Detail

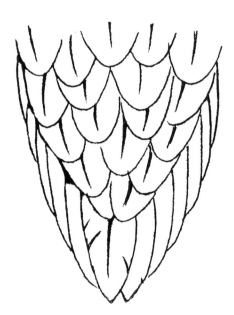

Upper Tail Detail

Illustrations by Frank Russell

Photocopy at 100%

American Woodcock patterns

INTERMEDIATE

Underbill

Top View

Feather Contours

Relief Carve a Whimsical House

By Jim Cline

INTERMEDIATE

I love to carve whimsical scenes in wood but hate the time it takes to prepare a relief carving for the detail stage using traditional methods. To solve this problem, I devised a way to block out the levels quickly using a rotary power carver equipped with a router attachment and spiral saw cutters to do most of the work. I discovered that if I use the cutters free-hand, I can create a unique texture that I have not been able to duplicate with any other tool.

Most of my carvings are made using construction-grade spruce and pine (2x12, 2x10, and 2x lumber). Because I'm not worried about messing up an expensive piece of wood, I experiment more and just carve away. I sell these pieces, which take me anywhere from 12 to 20 hours to carve, for up to $180. I can then turn around and spend that income on more wood and tools.

I prefer using power because the construction-grade lumber I use is hard to carve with hand tools. If you use basswood or something similar, you will get better results with hand tools. To carve in the different levels, I set my router attachment to the depth desired and block out the area with spiral saw cutters. Alternatively, you can use the spiral cutter to make a stop cut and clear the area out with a chisel.

NOTE: Spiral saw cutters are very aggressive. Using a Dremel with a router attachment instead of a router will help you gain some control. Practice this technique on a piece of scrap wood before beginning your carving.

Here are high-speed rotary power carvers and a router attachment.

INTERMEDIATE

1 **_Transfer the pattern to the work piece._** I slip a piece of carbon paper under the pattern and trace it onto the wood. Darken the perimeter of the pattern with a felt-tip marker to make it easier to rough out.

2 **_Clamp the blank securely._** Attach a hardwood stick to the back of the blank to clamp it with. The stick also gets the carving up and off the bench. Screw the stick to the carving in the two places marked with an *x* on the pattern.

3 **_Cut the perimeter and negative spaces._** I use a rotary saw tool. It takes a few passes to remove all of the waste wood. Don't forget the four small areas inside the outer perimeter. Clean up the sawdust with a shop vac.

4 **_Rough out the back of the carving._** Remove the clamping stick and attach it to the front. The area marked in black is to be removed. Take the area behind the smoke down ½" (1.3cm). Remove ¾" (1.9cm) of wood from behind the tree and the bottom left corner. Remove 1" (2.5cm) of wood from behind the bush.

5 **_Rough out the lowest levels on the front of the carving._** Reattach the hardwood stick to the back of the carving. Make several passes across the door, window, and moon. You want to carve away 1¼" (3.2cm) of wood in the parts marked in black on the project.

6 **_Carve down the walls of the house._** Use the spiral cutter to take ¾" (1.9cm) off the areas marked in black on the project. Leave the area at the tip of the smoke there to support the base of the cutter and remove the tip with a chisel afterward.

7 *Block in the next levels.* Use the spiral cutter to carve the doorstep and the rear tree leaves down 7⁄16" (1.1cm). I find it helpful to shade the entire section as a guide.

8 *Shape the roof and the tree trunk.* Take them down 5⁄16" (8mm) with the spiral cutter.

9 *Texture the leaves.* Use the spiral cutter free-hand in the rotary power carver to add short jagged lines for the leaves. Work from the outer edges in, and keep both hands on the tool.

10 *Undercut the window and door.* The window is undercut on all four sides, but don't undercut the bottom of the door. Use a 1⁄4" (6mm)-diameter ball-shaped carbide bur. Leave the wood about 1⁄8" (3mm)-thick after undercutting.

11 *Undercut the tree and leaves.* Use a 1⁄2"-diameter by 1⁄8"-thick (13mm by 3mm) disc-shaped carbide bur. Use this same bur to undercut between the chimney and the smoke and between the tree and the moon.

12 *Shape the chimney and roof.* Round the front face of the chimney and smoke. Use a knife or chisel. Then, round the outer edge of the roof and a small amount of the tree trunk.

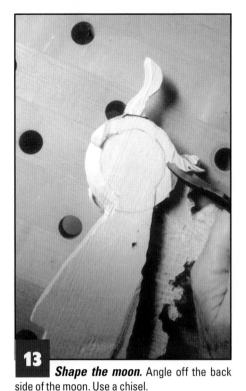

13 Shape the moon. Angle off the back side of the moon. Use a chisel.

14 Make the door and window. Trace the pattern for the window and door onto a piece of ⅛" (3mm)-thick scrap. Make the window oversized so you can glue it over the frame. Carve out the panes with a cone-shaped carbide bur. Trim the door to fit, and glue it in place.

15 Sand the carving. Use a sanding mandrel loaded with Swiss sandpaper to remove any burs and to smooth the surfaces. Start with 80 grit and use progressively finer grits up to 220 grit. Swiss sandpaper is more flexible and resists loading up when sanding the soft wood.

16 Attach a hanger to the back of the carving. Choose a place where the screws won't damage the front surface of the carving. Then, apply your finish of choice. I finish some of my carvings with a clear, satin, acrylic spray finish. If you use hardwood for your carving, boiled linseed oil mixed with turpentine is another option.

Materials & Tools

Materials
- Pine, 1½" (3.2cm) thick: 8" x 12" (20.3cm x 30.5cm)
- Scrap, 1" (2.5cm) thick: 1" x 10" (2.5cm x 25.4cm)
- Pine, ⅛" (3mm) thick: window, door, 1½" x 7" (3.2cm x 17.8cm)
- Saw-tooth hanger
- Sandpaper, Swiss: assorted grits
- Finish
- Carbon paper
- Wood glue

Tools
- Rotary power carver equipped with router attachment
- Spiral saw cutters for the power carver: assorted
- Carbide burs: ¼" (6mm)-dia. ball; small cone; ½"-dia. x ⅛"-thick (13mm x 3mm) disc
- Sanding mandrel
- Chisel
- Carving knife

Carving Safety

The rotary tool used most in this type of carving is a ⅛" (3mm) wood cutting bit. It can be used free-hand, but I suggest using it with an adjustable depth control or a router attachment.

If you do use it free-hand, the bit cuts very aggressively and may act like it has a mind of its own. It cuts best and is most controllable between 30,000 to 35,000 rpm. Just be cautious when using this tool. Keep the carving securely clamped down so you can use both hands on the tool. Replace the bit when it gets dull, and keep your body parts away from the moving bit.

Whimsical House patterns

Photocopy at 120% or desired size.

"For Sale" is another variation on the project illustrated here.

Walking Stick Wizard

By Frank Russell

A

B

Photocopy to desired size

Materials & Tools

Materials:
- Straight limb: any size
- Glue stick
- Natural staining oil
- Flat or matte lacquer or exterior-grade polyurethane
- Raw umber and Mars black acrylic paints (for antiquing wash) (optional)
- Metal or rubber cane tip (optional)

Tools:
- Band saw or scroll saw
- Small and medium flame-shaped carbide burs
- Small and medium flame-shaped ruby carver
- Medium bud-shaped ruby carver
- Small ball-shaped diamond bit
- Small flame-shaped diamond bit
- Medium inverted cone-shaped safe end diamond bit and small sharp inverted cone-shaped diamond bit
- Defuzzing mandrel or rotary bristle brush
- Small cylinder-shaped stone bit

A good straight limb from a tree can be used after removing the bark and seasoning, but for the purpose of this book, the stick part was turned on a lathe, and a carving block was left on top. Of course, the length, size, and shape of the block will depend on what you plan to carve on top of the walking stick.

I was certainly glad to see the end of the beard—I didn't think I'd ever care to texture hair again after I completed this project. I still haven't given the man a price who wants one with a little bigger head and a beard that winds all the way to the bottom!

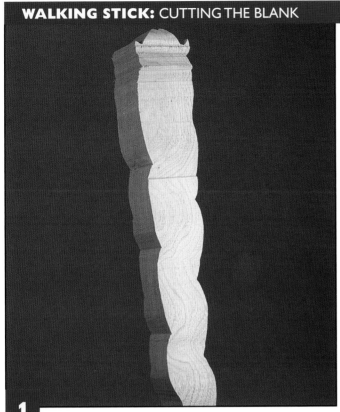

1 *Cut the blank two ways on the bandsaw.* I copy my drawings to the desired size on a photocopier, and then I use a glue stick to glue them directly to the stock while I saw along the drawn lines.

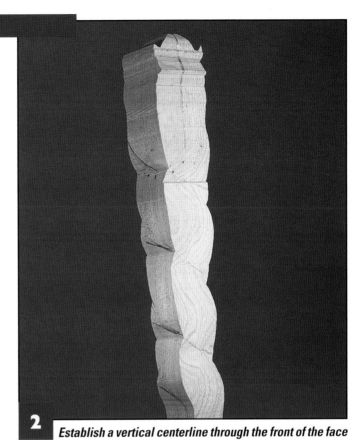

2 *Establish a vertical centerline through the front of the face area.* Draw any wasting or rough shaping lines over the entire blank.

3 *Rough shape entire carving.* Use a small and medium flame-shaped carbide bur.

4 *Shape contours of the face—eye mounds, nose, cheeks, and forehead.* Finish shape head hair and entire beard. Use medium flame-shaped and bud-shaped ruby carvers.

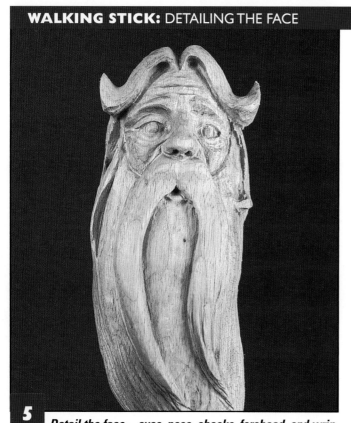

5 ***Detail the face—eyes, nose, cheeks, forehead, and wrinkles.*** Use the small flame-shaped ruby carver and small ball-shaped diamond bit for the nostril holes.

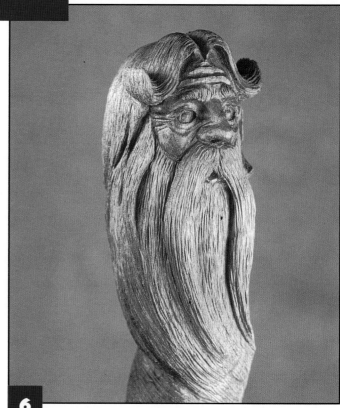

6 ***Texture the hair over entire piece.*** Use the medium inverted cone-shaped safe end diamond bit for the beard and hair; the small sharp inverted cone-shaped diamond bit where the beard and mustache meet the face; the small cylinder-shaped stone for the eyebrows; and the small flame-shaped diamond bit to clean up detail. Clean and defuzz with a defuzzing mandrel or rotary bristle brush.

WALKING STICK: FINISHING THE STICK

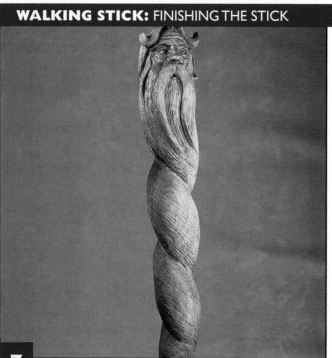

7 ***Finish.*** Touch up any details, clean with a rotary brush or defuzzer, and then enhance the grain with a natural staining oil. Allow to dry thoroughly. Finish with flat or matte lacquer or exterior-grade polyurethane. This project is for outdoor use and will undoubtedly see many miles.

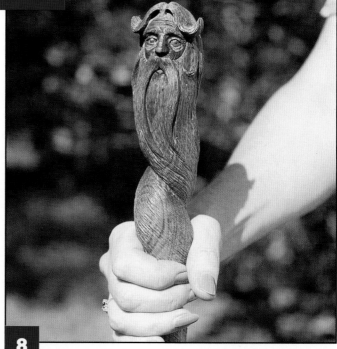

8 ***Add an antiquing wash.*** If greater depth is desired, wash raw umber/Mars black over the stick. This leaves residue in the depressions and enhances the carved detail. Seal the carving with two coats of exterior-grade finish. Finish the bottom with a metal cane stud and a rubber crutch tip.

INTERMEDIATE

Decorative Cardinal

By Frank Russell

Now we come to the most ornery piece of wood that I have ever carved. I had a piece of Spanish Cedar that a vendor friend had given me at a woodcarving show. Just to check it, I smoothed one corner and textured a few feathers on it. They textured beautifully, so I blanked out the cardinal that follows.

All went well until I got to the texturing sequence, and the struggle began from there on. The wood had annular rings that were unbelievable—the wide rings textured nicely, but the narrow rings were as soft as balsa, and were filled with a resinous substance that clogged a texturing bit very quickly.

I was within a heartbeat of throwing it out and starting all over again, but New England tenacity made me continue. After completing the carving portion of the bird, the surface was such that I decided to paint it as a decorative carving as opposed to a realistic bird carving. I merely highlighted color areas and allowed much of the reddish wood to show through.

Materials & Tools

Materials:
- Wood of choice
- Glass eye (optional)
- Acrylic lacquer, varnish, or fine-grade, water-based sanding sealer
- Acrylic paints: cadmium orange medium, cadmium orange light, Mars black, raw umber, burnt sienna, burnt umber, cadmium red medium, cadmium red light

Tools:
- Band saw
- Carbide bit: small flame-shaped
- Ruby bits: small flame-shaped, medium flame-shaped, small bud-shaped
- Stone bit: small inverted cone
- Diamond bit: small inverted cone
- Rotary bristle brush

ADVANCED

CARDINAL: ROUGHING OUT

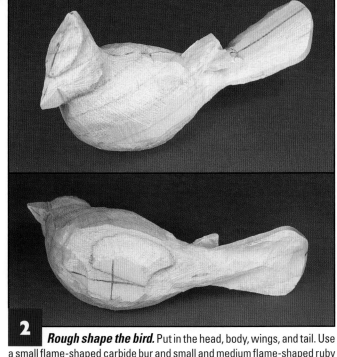

1 *Blank out the project on the bandsaw.* Draw a centerline all the way around the bird from tail to beak. Always honor your centerline. If you carve it away, draw it back in place again. Lay out the head and wings. Shape to these layout lines during the roughing out process.

2 *Rough shape the bird.* Put in the head, body, wings, and tail. Use a small flame-shaped carbide bur and small and medium flame-shaped ruby carvers.

CARDINAL: DEFINING FEATHER GROUPS

3 *Lay out the feather groups.* Make the cape, side feathers, cheeks, jowls, breast/bib indentations, and beak and eye location.

4 *Shape the feather groups.* Raise the cape away from the wing covert group, the coverts away from the wings, and one wing over the other. Separate the left side tail feathers from the right side by raising one away from the other. Use small and medium flame-shaped ruby carvers.

5 *Lay out individual feathers.* Indicate feathers that separate, overlaid feathers, and the direction of feathers. Draw lines to indicate the direction and turn the feathers will take. If these flow lines are pleasing to the eye, honor them as you texture by following in the same direction.

6 ***Relieve feather separations, feather overlays, individual feathers, and feather accents.*** On a real bird, some feathers break away from others, some lay over others, and some stand away by themselves. Carving these varieties into the feather pattern of your bird gives the carving a very pleasing effect. Don't overdo it or you will have a bird that looks as if it just flew through a turbine. Use small flame-shaped and small bud-shaped ruby carvers.

7 ***Next, texture the feathers on the entire bird.*** Texture from the rear forward and from the bottom upward. As you texture, occasionally allow a stroke to run down into the feather below if it is going in the same direction. This will give continuity and flow to the feather group. Use a small inverted cone stone bit, a small inverted cone diamond bit, and a rotary bristle brush for cleaning and defuzzing.

CARDINAL: FINISHING

CARDINAL: PAINTING THE BIRD

8 ***Seal carving.*** Use several thinned coats of acrylic lacquer or varnish or a fine-grade water-based sanding sealer. Allow the bird to dry thoroughly and then paint.

9 ***Paint.*** Paint the beak cadmium orange medium, highlighted with cadmium orange light. For the bib, use Mars black with raw umber. The irises are burnt sienna/burnt umber with Mars black/raw umber pupils. Paint the body feather highlights by dry brushing cadmium red medium with highlights of cadmium red light. Blend the outer feathers of the tail, wings, and wing coverts with a medium dark mixture of cadmium red medium and raw umber. Then, apply an antiquing wash to accentuate texturing highlights and major feather group indentations.

Decorative cardinal patterns

12 Tail Feathers

Optional Head Positions

ADVANCED

Undertail Detail

Underbill Detail

Tail Cross Section

Photocopy to desired size

Black Bear

By Wanda Marsh

ADVANCED

As an animal carver, I admit some of my best reference and inspiration comes from the Discovery Channel. I can not only view close-ups of the animals but also learn about their behaviors.

I saw enough videos and photographs of bears on rocks, especially ones preying on salmon, to know the pose I chose for this project would be enjoyed by other carvers. I kept the base and overall size compact because large pieces of wood, in this case basswood, are expensive, and when wood has to be laminated to obtain a big block, the cost is driven up considerably.

Power Carving

Whether I am working on animals or flowers, I rely on power carving tools. For roughing out the bear, I was able to remove wood very quickly with the aid of carbide cutters. To define some separation between the bear's paws and the rocks—the composition is carved from a single block of wood—I turned to fine diamond bits and ruby carvers.

For texturing the bear, I put several sizes of diamond discs to work. In less than three hours, I haired the entire animal. I also went over the texturing lines with a burning pen. The burn provides an extra tone, making the hair more realistic after paints are applied.

After roughing out, fine detailing, texturing, and burning, I still was not finished with the power tools. Because bits and burs tend to raise fuzzy grain in basswood, I cleaned up the bear with a rotary defuzzer.

Rocks are scarce in my area of Texas, so I purchased some from a garden center for reference. If you study a variety of rocks, you will find much more than meets the eye after a casual glance. Not only are there many textures, but there are also a variety of colors, especially earth tones, which happen to complement the bear. When carving the rocks, I took one extra step: I used hand tools to create and accentuate facets. If you sell power carved projects, you may have discovered some customers prefer a hand carved look and believe the piece is more valuable.

Painting Instructions

The process of painting the rocks tends to get messy, so start with them rather than the bear. Do not worry about minor problems such as an unpainted crevice. These can be corrected even after the bear is painted.

I prefer acrylic paints. They mix and blend well. Assemble the following colors, many of which are earth tones, and make a watery wash of each:

Burnt sienna
Burnt umber
Cadmium red
Charcoal black
Raw sienna
Raw umber
White

The secret to painting rocks is taking a "blotchy" approach while having the colors run together. Using the brush with a careless stroke, apply one color, then paint over it. Because there is no clear division of colors, neatness is not a priority. Do not bother to clean the brush as you change colors.

Some of the rocks should have more of one color than another. A very dark rock, for example, is base-colored in black with white applied sparingly. A brown rock is mostly raw umber with raw sienna highlights.

Photocopy to desired size

Black bear patterns

After applying at least two colors to each rock, spatter them with all of the colors listed above. To accomplish this, dip an old toothbrush into the washes. Pull a fingernail or the side of a pencil across the wet bristles to affect the spatter. Try out the painting process on scrap wood before tackling the project.

Before painting the bear, realize you do not want to cover the texturing and burn lines, which a heavy coat of paint will do. Instead, use several light washes of each color or mix.

Start with the muzzle by applying a mixture of white and raw sienna. Make sure this wash fades into the raw umber used for the rest of the body. To paint shadow areas—creases and the underside of the animal—add a small amount of black to the raw umber. To create a shadow around the nose and mouth, use a small amount of raw umber and black mixed together. Apply it with a dry brush.

For the eyes, take black straight from the tube, applying the paint in a nice even coat. Let it thoroughly dry. Next, mix raw umber and white to make a light brown tone for the irises. Let the paint dry. Paint the pupils black and let them completely dry. Paint a fine highlight or spot on the eyes using white from the tube. Finally, brush on a small line of cadmium red beside the pupils.

After the carving is completely dry, seal the carving with two to three coats of matte finish. Let each coat completely dry before spraying the next coat.

Mix together a small amount of five-minute epoxy, and with a toothpick, apply a dot to the center of each eye. Only a small amount is needed to cover the eyes. To keep the realistic look at its best, do not get any of the epoxy into the eye creases. When the adhesive is dry, carving fans will think that glass eyes were inserted.

Black bear patterns

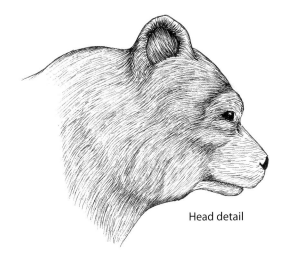

Head detail

Photocopy to desired size

Illustrations by Jack Kochan

Creating a Musical Mouse

Customize this playful design for the musician in your life

By Doug Brooks

I started the Mice-Tro collection by carving a small mouse and pairing him with a bass fiddle. I took some liberties with the shape of the instrument to add movement and show that the mouse is bending notes. I had so much fun with the project, I went on to create an entire band, including the lead Mice-Tro, or maestro, who keeps everyone in tune.

This little critter makes a great gift for musicians. Change the instrument and pose of the mouse to suit your needs. I hope you have as much fun as I did and end up creating an entire band.

Doug Brooks created an entire band of note-bending mice led by a maestro. Doug dubbed the caricatures his *Mice-Tro* collection.

1 ***Rough out the bass fiddle.*** Transfer the front-view pattern to the fiddle blank. Cut the front profile on a band saw. Transfer the side-view pattern onto the blank and cut the side profile.

2 ***Carve the fiddle.*** Mark the areas to remove. Sketch in the rough details and use a knife or rotary-power carver with aggressive carving bits to shape the arm, the body, and the string anchor. Then, sand the fiddle to remove any tool marks.

3 ***Woodburn the major landmarks.*** Draw in the details and trace along the lines with a woodburner. In addition to being elements of the finished carving, some of these burned lines act as shallow stop cuts.

4 ***Finish shaping the fiddle.*** Use a small cylinder-shaped diamond bit in a micro motor or your tool of choice. Use the wood-burned lines as stop cuts. Don't be afraid to get creative with the shape and details.

5 ***Add the string bridge.*** Carve the string bridge from a separate piece of wood. Carve a small groove for the bridge in the fiddle body and glue the bridge in place. Then, carve the sound holes into the fiddle body.

ADVANCED

6 ***Prepare the tuning keys.*** Drill four ¹⁄₁₆" (2mm)-diameter holes into a ⅛" (3mm)-diameter dowel. Glue round toothpicks into the holes. Slice the dowel into four pieces. Trim the toothpick flush on one side of the dowel and ³⁄₁₆" (5mm) from the dowel on the opposite side.

7 ***Finish the tuning keys.*** Shape the dowel pieces to resemble tuning keys. Drill ¹⁄₁₆" (2mm)-diameter holes for the keys into the arm of the fiddle. Dry fit the keys and make any necessary adjustments. Remove the keys and paint them black.

MOUSE: ROUGHING OUT THE MOUSE

8 ***Rough out the mouse.*** Transfer the side-view pattern onto the mouse blank and cut the side profile on a band saw. Then, transfer the front-view pattern onto the blank and cut the front profile.

9 ***Carve the head.*** Draw centerlines on the blank and shade the waste areas to be carved away. Remove the wood using your tools of choice. I use a rotary-power carver. Redraw the centerlines as needed.

10 ***Shape the body.*** Mark the areas to remove, using the pattern and carved fiddle as a guide. Use your tools of choice to shape the arms, belly, and back. Draw the shape of the feet on the bottom of the blank. Use caution as you shape the feet because you are working with end grain.

MOUSE: REFINING THE MOUSE

11 ***Refine the carving.*** I use diamond bits in a variety of shapes. Smooth the inside of the ears, and carve the eyes and fingers. Outline the eyes and fingers with a woodburner.

12 ***Add the fur texture.*** Use a cone-shaped bit in a rotary-power carver. Then, carve the tail and carve an area to insert the tail into the mouse. Glue the tail in place.

13 ***Dry fit the mouse with the fiddle.*** Dry fit the mouse to the fiddle and determine the best position. Then, create a base for the carving.

MOUSE: FINISHING THE CARVING

14 ***Paint the carving.*** I use oil paints, but acrylic paints will work as well. Create a mixture of burnt umber, burnt sienna, and warm white for the mouse brown. The belly is warm white. The ears, tail, mouth, and paws are pink. The neck, string tuners, and string anchor are black. I use a dark stain for the fiddle.

15 ***Attach the carvings to the base.*** Allow the paint and finish to dry. Inspect the pieces from all different angles and make sure everything meets your approval. Use a push pin to make three holes on each side of the nose. Glue bristles from a push broom in the holes to create whiskers. Glue the mouse and fiddle in place on the base. Glue the keys into the fiddle arm.

Materials & Tools

Materials:
- Basswood, 2" (5.1cm) square: mouse, 3¼" (8.3cm) long
- Basswood, 2½" (6.4cm) thick: bass fiddle, tail, 3" x 6" (7.6cm x 15.2cm)
- Scraps of basswood (string bridge)
- Dowel, ⅛" (3mm) dia.: tuning keys, 3" (7.6cm) long
- Toothpicks: round (tuning keys)
- Oil or acrylic paint: burnt umber, burnt sienna, warm white, pink, black
- Stain: dark (bass fiddle)
- Wood glue
- Sandpaper: assorted grits
- Bristles from a soft push broom: 6 (whiskers)

Tools:
- Band saw
- Carving knife
- Rotary-power carver
- Aggressive power carving bits
- Drum sander
- Woodburner and pens/tips
- Micro motor rotary-power carver
- Diamond bits: small cylinder-shaped; assorted
- Stone bit: cone shaped
- Drill with assorted small bits
- Push pin (to make whisker holes)

Designing Different Band Members

Start by carving the instrument. Then, make a cardboard template of the mouse. Cut the arms and legs separately and pin them in place at the joints. Position the limbs to fit the instrument, and then trace around the template to create a pattern for the mouse.

Musical mouse patterns

Tail

Grain direction

String bridge

Contributors

Dave Arndt
Dave Arndt is retired and lives in Saginaw, Mich., with his wife, Denise. Dave is a member and past president of the Tri City Carvers Club and has been carving decorative fish for more than 15 years.

Doug Brooks
Doug Brooks, who resides in Bobcaygeon, Ont., Canada, spends most of his time in the home-based workshop attached to his studio. A fine-art painter and graphic artist, Doug took up carving in 1999 as a hobby without deadlines. His quirky sense of humor comes out in his wooden creations, especially as a release after spending time on a serious piece for competition.

Steve Buchholz
Steve Buchholz of Kettle Falls, Wash., has been carving for many years. He grew up watching his father carve award-winning decorative birds, and eventually began carving himself. Locally, he is called the "Stick Guy" because of the vast number of walking sticks he has carved. Contact Steve at *stickguy52@hotmail.com*.

Jim Cline
Jim Cline took up woodcarving when he retired in 1987, has taken home a number of ribbons, and has taught woodcarving at the Naramata Center in Canada.

Lori Corbett
Lori Corbett has been carving since 1986 and offers classes in bird carving at her studio in St. Anthony, Idaho, where she resides with her husband. *www.whisperingeagle.com*.

Keith Dalton
A Tennessee native, Keith Dalton was born and raised in the Smokey Mountains. Although his father was a carver, Keith only started carving in 2002. He prefers power carving animals, but will occasionally carve with hand tools. Keith has won numerous blue ribbons at shows in the Southeast. A retired brick layer, Keith lives in Seymour, Tenn., with his wife, Becky.

Lynn Diel
A carver who enjoys designing his own very affordable carving tools and accessories, Lynn Diel was the winner of *WCI's* first Poor Man's Tool Contest held in 1998.

Frank Foust
An experienced woodworker, Frank Foust has built projects ranging from children's furniture to his own home. As a volunteer, he's helped repair and rebuild churches in the United States and Central America.

Jack Kochan
Jack Kochan has been a frequent contributor to and illustrator for *Woodcarving Illustrated* and makes his home in Leesport, Pennsylvania.

Rob Lucero
Rob Lucero is the owner of Ruby Wood Art. For more of his work, visit his website at *www.RubyWoodArt.com*.

Wanda Marsh
Wanda Marsh is a professional carver, author, and instructor who lives with her husband in New Caney, Texas.

Keoma McCaffrey
Keoma McCaffrey lives in Northern California with her husband, Jeff, and sons. She carves most of her work from salvaged local hardwoods.

Frank Russell
Frank is an 11th generation Vermonter from a long line of diverse artisans and craftsmen. He has won many carving competitions both in the United States and Canada, and has judged at numerous shows, including the Ward Foundation World Competition in Ocean City, MD.

Chuck Solomon and Dave Hamilton
Chuck Solomon and Dave Hamilton are avid carvers and instructors and have co-authored several books together.

Jose Valencia
Jose Valencia is one of the top gunstock carvers in the United States and was the Western Art Rodeo Association Carving Champion in 2011. As one of Profitable Hobbies' Master Carvers, Jose teaches classes in his studio in Phoenix, Ariz. He has published a book, *Carving Gunstocks: Power Techniques*. For more of his work, visit *www.JoseValenciaStudio.com*.

Kenny Vermillion
Kenny Vermillion has been carving wildlife subjects professionally since 1983. His works have won hundreds of awards and are in private and museum collections throughout the U.S. and seven other countries. *www.kennyvermillion.com*.

Index

Note: Page numbers in *italics* indicate projects.